A Faith of Your Own

Also from Westminster John Knox Press
by Ronald J. Allen:

The Life of Jesus for Today
Preaching without Prejudice: A Three-Volume Lectionary Commentary
  (with Clark M. Williamson)
Preaching Is Believing: The Sermon as Theological Reflection
Preaching Verse by Verse (with Gilbert Leinbach Bartholomew)
Preaching the Topical Sermon
The Teaching Minister (with Clark M. Williamson)

A Faith of Your Own

Naming What You Really Believe

Ronald J. Allen

WESTMINSTER
JOHN KNOX PRESS
LOUISVILLE · KENTUCKY

First edition
Published by Westminster John Knox Press
Louisville, Kentucky

10 11 12 13 14 15 16 17 18 19—10 9 8 7 6 5 4 3 2 1

Unless otherwise indicated, Scripture quotations are from the New Revised Standard Version of the Bible, copyright © 1989 by the Division of Christian Education of the National Council of the Churches of Christ in the U.S.A., and are used by permission.

Book design by Drew Stevens
Cover design by designpointinc.com

Library of Congress Cataloging-in-Publication Data

Allen, Ronald J. (Ronald James).
    A faith of your own : naming what you really believe / Ronald J. Allen.
        p. cm.
    Includes bibliographical references.
    ISBN 978-0-664-23365-5 (alk. paper)
    1. Theology, Doctrinal—Popular works. 2. Identification (Religion) I. Title.
    BT77.A43 2010
    230—dc22

                                                                2009028351

PRINTED IN THE UNITED STATES OF AMERICA

♾ The paper used in this publication meets the minimum requirements
of the American National Standard for Information Sciences—Permanence of Paper
for Printed Library Materials, ANSI Z39.48-1992

Westminster John Knox Press advocates the responsible use of our natural resources.
The text paper of this book is made from 30% post-consumer waste.

Contents

Introduction

I was leading a Bible study in a local congregation and our focus was on a passage of Scripture that presented a particular view of Jesus Christ. A layperson tentatively raised a hand and said, "I am troubled by this image of Jesus . . . [long pause, and then, tentatively] . . . Do I have to believe it?" Without intentionally thinking through my response, I reported that the New Testament itself contains multiple interpretations of Jesus, and the history of the church produced even more. I summarized several prominent pictures, and briefly indicated my own stance and why I hold it. The person who had raised the question leading to this discussion again put up a hand. "I've never heard this kind of explanation before. I didn't know it was possible to believe these other ways. . . . [Another pause] . . . Now I have to figure out what *I* really believe."

THE PURPOSE: TO HELP YOU NAME
A FAITH OF YOUR OWN

When leading this Bible study, I stumbled into a way of helping laypeople come to greater clarity about what they *really* can believe. Using a similar approach over several years in many local congregations, I have found that people often identify their own deepest convictions when exposed to multiple ways of understanding God, Christ, the Holy Spirit, and other key elements of Christian faith. This book takes that approach for people who want to name a faith of their own in dialogue with multiple possibilities.

Few Christians arrive at a set of beliefs that they can then set in stone for the rest of their lives. What we believe evolves in response to insights into the Bible, to questions, to changes in life circumstances, or to things that happen in the larger world. A faith is a living thing. Nevertheless, Christians often find it helpful to identify what they can most fully believe at a given moment. Such moments of recognition can both empower the present and lead us toward the future. Such a moment can also be a milepost from which to gauge further developments.

Most books of this kind seek to persuade readers that one particular interpretation of Christian faith is the best one. By contrast, this volume surveys possibilities for belief without trying to insist that one particular viewpoint is the true one. Of course, my proclivities are evident, but I try to present all perspectives clearly and respectfully. Readers have to choose what notions (here or elsewhere) make the most sense to them.

THE CONTENTS OF THIS BOOK

This book is divided into nine chapters, each focusing on a topic central to Christian faith.[1] Chapter 1 deals with the background issue of the resources we use when developing a faith. Subsequent chapters focus on specific core elements: God, Jesus, the Holy Spirit, the Trinity, God's ultimate purposes, what the church is to be and do, evil, and Christianity and other religions. This list is not comprehensive but it does cover basic issues.

Each chapter follows a similar format. The first section sets out leading ways the topic is understood in the Bible. The second section identifies important ways the church has interpreted the topic in our history since the Bible. The third section lifts up contemporary perspectives. The reader can then make a judgment as to which viewpoints seem more and which less persuasive. The chapters end with questions for reflection that can be used by individuals or small groups.

I try to write in everyday English. Occasionally, I introduce and explain a word from the rarefied language of academic discourse.[2] This book does not contain a lot of scholarly apparatus such as footnotes and quotations as I have drawn mainly on ideas that are commonplace in Christian circles.

WHAT IS AT STAKE?

Why is it important to be clear about what we believe (and what we do not)? Because what we believe determines not only how we see God, ourselves, others, and the world, but also what we expect from God and from ourselves and from the world. What we believe determines how we pray and how we act. When I pray, for instance, what can I count on God to do? Moreover, what we believe shapes the kind of world for which we work. When we lie dying, what we believe determines how we approach what comes next.

We tend to become like the things that we believe. Indeed, we often embody what we believe. If we believe in a large, loving, compassionate, generous God, then we become large, loving, compassionate, and generous people. If we believe in a small, rigid, legalistic God, then we tend to become small, rigid, and legalistic.

By the end of this book, I hope you will be able to articulate your own deepest convictions. With a clear set of convictions in hand, you can compare and contrast your faith with that of others. You can develop a sense of where you connect with others, and where you differ from them. You can get a sense of what is compelling about your faith, and where you continue to have questions. But a faith is not something you put in a box and tape shut. As already noted, a faith is a living set of relationships and ideas that sometimes change in response to new circumstances.

MORE THAN CREATING A FAITH IN YOUR OWN IMAGE

A friend with whom I discussed this book pointed to a possible unintended consequence. "It sounds as if you are setting up a cafeteria line of beliefs so that people can go through and pick up a faith they like. People can just create faith in their own images." I reply in three ways.

First, the Bible itself does something similar by letting different theological viewpoints sit alongside one another, implicitly putting the reader in the position of having to identify the perspectives that make more and less sense. Indeed, the different thinkers in the Bible sometimes critique one another.

Second, statements of doctrine, theology, or faith are always matters of interpretation. This book encourages laypeople to recognize possibilities, to compare and contrast them, and to select the one(s) that are most promising.

Third, this book seeks to raise the process of naming a faith to a conscious, self-aware level and to recognize what we gain and what we lose by making different choices. These pages encourage a broad range of our conversation partners so that we are not limited to talking with ourselves. Conversation with the Bible, with Christian tradition, and with interpreters in our own world can enrich the conversation so that what we believe is more than rote reflection of the Bible, tradition, or our present values and behaviors.

AWARENESS THAT IS HARD TO NAME:
FEELING AND INTUITION

This book urges you to name—as specifically as possible—your deepest religious convictions. It pushes you toward perception at the conscious level, but it cannot address awareness at the levels of intuition and feeling. On the one hand, there are dimensions of life that are deeper than our conscious verbal awareness. As a friend of mine entitled a book, we have knowledge that is *Too Deep for Words.*[3]

On the other hand, my impression is that many people use the realm of feeling as an excuse to quit thinking before they have really tried to work through an issue. In Bible study classes, for example, people often get to the edge of a difficult issue and say, "Oh, that idea is a mystery. We cannot understand it." Not long ago, I asked a student why that student believed a certain thing, and the student said, "I know that I know that I know." This student had a feeling, and that was the end of the discussion. But the student had the capability of thinking much more deeply about the subject, and I tried to push the student toward deeper theological water. There are moments in life when intuition and feeling are not enough. We need to know what we believe and why we believe that way. In a similar way, this little book tries to help you say more clearly what you believe and why you believe it.

1

Resources for Developing a Faith

Before jumping into the content of what we believe, a prior matter comes to the surface: How do we develop a faith? What are the sources of what we believe? How do we work with those sources to articulate a faith that is compelling?

My colleague Helene Russell uses the expression "embedded faith" or "embedded theology" to speak of the beliefs that most people take for granted. As you begin reading this book, you have some ideas about God, Christ, the Holy Spirit, the church, and the world. Some of these ideas may have come from the Bible and the teaching of the church, while others may have come from places as diverse as a media preacher, local religious customs, or conversation at a coffee klatch. Ideas from such sources become embedded in your mind and heart.

The agenda of this chapter is to identify the sources that people in the world of the Bible and in the church have most often used to clarify what they believe. You will probably recognize some ideas from your embedded theology, but you may also discover some resources you had not considered or may get a fresh angle of vision on some resources you have known and used.

SOURCES OF RELIGIOUS INSIGHT
IN THE WORLD OF THE BIBLE

The church has often said that the Bible is our most important source of religious insight. Less often noticed is the fact that within the world of the Bible, people drew on different resources for understanding God and life. Three are particularly important: direct communication from God, wisdom, and tradition.

Direct Communication from God

The Bible pictures God (or representatives from God) communicating directly with people. This scenario occurs in both the Old and New Testaments. Such a picture first occurs in the Bible in Genesis 3:8–19, when God spoke with Eve and Adam in the Garden of Eden much as one person speaks with another, to confront them with the fact that, by eating the forbidden fruit, they had violated God's one prohibition. Biblical authors indicate that the word of God came to particular people such as Jonah, Micah, and Zechariah (Jonah 1:1; Mic. 1:1; Zech. 1:1). At the baptism God spoke directly from heaven: "This is my Son, the Beloved, with whom I am well pleased" (Matt. 3:17).

The Bible also portrays God communicating directly with people through dreams and visions. For example, at the age of seventeen, Joseph dreamed of his future relationship with his siblings (Gen. 37:4–11). In the book of Acts, Cornelius and Peter have a double vision. The Gentile Cornelius is told to send for Peter. The next day, Peter received a vision of a large sheet containing both clean and unclean creatures and the command, "Get up, Peter; kill and eat" (Acts 10:1–16).

The biblical writers sometimes portray the Holy Spirit communicating directly with people. The Old Testament speaks of the Spirit "coming upon" people and directing them (e.g., Judg. 3:10; 2 Chr. 15:1). The Spirit anointed both the words and actions of Isaiah and Jesus (Isa. 61:1; Luke 4:18–19). The Spirit spoke through tongues at Corinth (1 Cor. 14:1–5) and gave the book of Revelation to the prophet John (Rev. 1:10; 4:2).

Today's reader may think that the ancient community unquestioningly accepted all such things. First John, however, cautions, "Beloved, do not believe every spirit, but test the spirits to see whether they are from God; for many false prophets have gone out into the world"

(1 John 4:1). The community should not simply accept such messages, but should test the degree to which they seem authentic.

Awareness That Arises from Reflection on Experience (Wisdom)

In the Bible, the wisdom tradition is centered in the books of Proverbs, Job, and Ecclesiastes. The materials assume that God planted clues to the divine purpose in nature and in life experience. God implanted the wisdom needed to know God's character and designs. We can discover the divine purposes by reflecting upon nature or upon experience.[1] Proverbs admonishes, "Go to the ant, you lazybones; consider its ways, and be wise" (Prov. 6:6). The industry of the ant is a model for the human being.

Parents were to teach wisdom at home, and sages (wisdom teachers) taught wisdom in schools. For example, the writer of Proverb exhorts, "Hear, my child, your father's instruction, and do not reject your mother's teaching" (Prov. 1:8). "The teaching of the wise is a fountain of life" (Prov. 13:14).

Some wisdom writings evaluate traditional teaching according to real life experience and conclude that the tradition is mistaken. The book of Deuteronomy, for instance, teaches that the obedient are blessed and the disobedient are cursed. The book of Job charges that this way of thinking is oversimplified. When the book of Job begins, Job is blameless, but through no disobedience on his part, Job's life collapses. One point of the book is that in real life experience, we observe that the obedient sometimes suffer for reasons not of their own making. Experience calls a conventional theological affirmation into question.

Discerning God's Purposes through Dialogue with Traditions

People in the world of the Bible most often turned to sacred traditions to help name God's presence and purposes. They did not have the complete Bible as we know it, but communities in those days often regarded particular traditions as reliable guides.[2] For example, before the exile, the people of Israel had come to regard the stories of Sarah and Abraham and their children, the narrative of the exodus and the making the covenant at Sinai and the entry into the promised land as pivotal traditions.

Later generations drew on these traditions to make theological sense of their situations. Isaiah, for instance, interpreted the return from the exile as a second exodus (Isa. 43:14–21). When faced with a group in Corinth who did not believe in a future resurrection or final judgment, Paul cited one of the oldest traditions about Jesus as the basis for pleading with the Corinthians to recognize that they too can be raised if they live faithfully and ethically in the present (1 Cor. 15:3–4). As we see in Matthew 5:17–20, the Law and the Prophets were widely regarded as authoritative in Jewish life.

A key point, however, is that the biblical communities did not just apply traditions from one generation to the next but interpreted the traditions. Jeremiah and the leaders of the temple, for instance, had competing interpretations of the covenant (Jer. 7:1–8:3; 26:1–6). At the time of Jesus, rabbi (teacher) Hillel said the grounds for divorce were liberal, whereas rabbi Shammai said that divorce was permissible only because of sexual infidelity. Mark portrays Jesus forbidding divorce altogether (Mark 10:1–12).

In the biblical period, interpreters sometimes differed with the tradition. Matthew adapts Mark's teaching on divorce to allow divorce on the grounds of unchastity (Matt. 5:27–30). Prior to Ezekiel, a common teaching was "The parents have eaten sour grapes, and the children's teeth are set on edge," meaning that the curse upon one generation for violating the covenant would be passed to subsequent generations. Ezekiel, however, concluded that that proverb "shall no longer be used in the land of Israel." Instead, "It is only the person who sins that shall die" (Ezek. 18:1–4). Within the world of the Bible itself, then, tradition was not a fixed deposit, but was a starting point for communities in each generation to converse regarding how they should understand God's purposes in their moment.

SOURCES OF RELIGIOUS INSIGHT IN THE HISTORY OF THE CHURCH

From the time of the Bible to the Enlightenment in the late 1700s and early 1800s, the church turned for religious insight to the traditions of the church, the Bible, philosophy, general experience, and direct communication.

Church Traditions

I begin with traditions rather than the Bible because many Christians functionally regard tradition as more authoritative than the Bible. Even if they do not say so directly, many people read the Bible through their traditions. I speak in the plural, "traditions," to emphasize that the church has always been a community of multiple (and sometimes differing) voices.

The largest single voice in the Western church is represented by the tradition extending from the Apostles' Affirmation (or Creed) (second century CE) to the Nicene Affirmation (325 and 381 CE) and the Chalcedonian formulation (451 CE). Councils of the church thus set out what they thought congregations must believe concerning God, Christ, the Spirit, the church, and other elements of Christian life.

Even churches that do not formally use these statements often regard the faith that they summarize as normative. Yet in every generation (including our own), leaders of the church need to explain and even defend these materials. These affirmations can be interpreted in multiple ways. Thus it is not enough simply to say, "I believe in the faith summarized in the Apostles' Affirmation of Faith." One must specify what it means to say, as in the Nicene Affirmation, "We believe in one God." One must specify what it means to say, "I [We] believe in one Lord, Jesus Christ." Some Christians take exception to elements of these affirmations.

Furthermore, most Christian movements have developed their own particular affirmations of faith, nearly always in line with tradition set in motion by the Apostles' Affirmation of Faith. For example, many Roman Catholic parishes regard the Catechism of the Catholic Church (1994) as a summary of Catholic doctrine. Many Reformed churches regard the Westminster Shorter Catechism (1647) in much the same way. However, contemporary Presbyterians continue to interpret the meaning of this and other historic affirmations of the Reformed traditions. Some churches eschew official affirmations of faith but still have traditions that informally function as authoritative.

Readers of this book need to become aware of the historic traditions that lie behind their own church. To what degree do you draw on the official and unofficial aspects of your tradition in voicing your own faith?

The Bible

The Bible is the one source to which virtually all Christians turn for insight into what to believe. The Bible contains stories that are fundamental to Christian identity and give the church much of its language. Many Christians want a faith anchored in the Bible. For example, perhaps the most important notion to my own faith is that God is love. I discovered this idea in the Bible. Church teaching helped me understand it more fully.

At key moments in the history of the church, the Bible has sparked renewal. For instance, Martin Luther's rediscovery of the doctrine of justification by grace alone began the Protestant Reformation.

However, using the Bible as a source was not (and is not) always as simple as it sounds. With the help of the image of a time line, we can see a complicating factor. The last of the Bible books were written about 110 CE. The traditions of the church continued to develop. The church often stood in its present and looked back to the Bible *through* the lens of church doctrine or some other concern. For example, many churches interpreted the Bible through the Apostles' and Nicene Affirmations of Faith. Instead of listening to the Bible in its own voice, people in the church sometimes read later church doctrine in the Affirmations into the Bible.

We can see this process in the histories of many churches. For example, the Roman Catholic Church has always drawn on the Bible as a guide, but has often regarded the doctrine of the church as the guide to reading the Bible. While Luther professed that the Bible alone should be the source of the church's faith, the Lutheran Church formulated the heart of its faith in the Heidelberg Catechism (1563), and today many Lutherans use that catechism as a window into the Bible. Even churches that do not subscribe to formal affirmations of faith (such as my own Christian Church [Disciples of Christ]) read the Bible through informal doctrinal ideas.

Moreover, in the history of the church, and today, Christians sometimes find certain parts of the Bible more appealing or instructive than others. For example, the prophets Isaiah and Micah declare that God will cause the peoples to "beat their swords into plowshares" (Isa. 2:4; Mic. 4:3). Joel, however, advises the nations to "beat your plowshares into swords" to serve as agents of God's judgment (Joel 3:10). The first saying is a staple of Christian consciousness. I do not ever remember hearing the latter cited in a Christian assembly. Here the church prefers one part of the Bible to another.

Philosophy

Philosophy is a source for understanding what the church believes, especially what the church believes about God. During the period of the Bible, Jewish and Christian writers made some use of Greek philosophical concepts, but the core of biblical ideas originated in Jewish thought. As the church moved into the Gentile sphere, the church's leaders increasingly drew on Greek philosophy, especially Plato and Aristotle, to help explain Christian faith. Indeed, some Christian writers essentially translated the Christian message into categories of Greek philosophy. For example, some Christians presented God as an Unmoved Mover along the lines of Aristotle's philosophy.

On the one hand, this development had the effect of helping people in Greek culture more readily understand and embrace Christian faith. On the other hand, interpreting Christian doctrine in Greek categories did change some core Christian ideas.

God Reveals God's Purposes in Nature (Natural Theology)

Some Christians believed that the capacity to understand things of God lies naturally within the human mind and is present in nature, where the human mind can observe it. While this line of reasoning is similar to that of the wisdom tradition in the Bible, those who follow it often ground their perspective more philosophically than biblically. Its most famous proponent, Thomas Aquinas (1225–1274 CE), drew heavily on Aristotle to argue that human beings were born with the natural ability to understand important religious themes without special revelation, and that the human community can establish truth through reason. On the basis of reason, for example, people can deduce that God exists. A community can have confidence that its thoughts concerning God and the world are reliable when those ideas cohere with the Bible and the tradition of the church. But natural theology cannot provide the community with awareness of the nuances of Christian doctrine and life. Natural theology, for instance, cannot alert human beings to the doctrine of the Trinity.

In the history of the church—and today—some Christians resisted the idea of natural theology. They have claimed that the world (including the human mind) is so stained by sin that we can trust only sources of religious insight that God has revealed, the most reliable of which is the Bible, followed by orthodox Christian teaching.

Nevertheless, even those who reject natural theology in favor of revealed theology hold that one's beliefs must be internally consistent. A faith cannot contradict itself.

Direct Communication from God

Some people in the history of the church, such as mystics, believed that they received direct revelations from God. Catherine of Siena (1347–80 CE), for example, went into the cloister, where she had a series of visions of hell and heaven that pointed to universal salvation. She believed that God told her to leave the monastery and take up a public ministry. Except for movements like the Society of Friends (Quakers) for whom direct communication is central, people in the history of the church largely regarded direct communication as unusual. In fact, some people did not recognize the validity of claims to direct communication from God.

SOURCES OF RELIGIOUS INSIGHT TODAY

In the contemporary era, we continue to find the Bible, tradition, direct communication, and experience as partners in the search for an authentic faith, while adding the scientific worldview and popular religion.

The Bible

Most people in the Christian movement these days believe that the Bible contains valuable perspectives on God and the religious life. But people have different understandings of the Bible and how to use it. Today's believers need to know where they stand, because the different perspectives call for using the Bible in different ways.

Some people (religious conservatives, sometimes known as fundamentalists and evangelicals) believe (a) that God inspired the Bible, (b) that all the contents of the Bible are internally consistent, and (c) that the contents of the Bible are universally valid in every time and place. Those who want to draw from the Bible need simply to understand what the Bible says and then to apply it to today.

Others (sometimes known as progressives) think that human beings wrote the biblical materials to interpret the divine presence and leading. They regard the Bible less as a single book and more as a library of different interpretations. They see the biblical authors as writing to their own particular moments in history. Consequently, when using the Bible, today's interpreter needs to sort through the elements in a biblical passage that may have lasting value and elements that were important in the ancient world but that are less so (or not so) today.

I have found that a lot of laypeople seek a viewpoint somewhere between these two poles. However, as a friend said, "This middle position is just too muddy." Most people incline more toward either the conservative or the progressive position.

In Bible study groups, I encounter people who do not have a clear idea of the nature of the Bible or how to use it. They have the feeling they should respect the Bible. They would like to think the Bible agrees with them on religious and ethical matters. They may know a few passages or verses or phrases, but they do not know how to bring those materials into dialogue with the church today.

Some people today disregard the Bible because they view it as hopelessly antiquated or as permeated with male superiority, slavery, tribalism, violence, and other abusive elements.

Tradition

Some in the church continue to regard the orthodox Christian tradition represented by the Apostles' Affirmation of Faith as tightly defining what Christians must believe. People in this tradition claim this faith as their own.

Others regard the tradition represented by the Apostles' Affirmation as containing wisdom that needs to be updated in expression and (for some) even in theological content. Consequently, in the last forty years many churches that use affirmations of faith have brought out new statements. For instance, in 1983, the Presbyterian Church (U.S.A.) brought out "A Brief Statement of Faith."

Quite a few people in our time long for connection with historic expressions of Christian faith. Thus, we find interest in churches with historic liturgies and dress, walking the labyrinth, and following the Christian year (Advent, Christmas, Epiphany, Lent, Easter, Pentecost, Ordinary Time). A movement has arisen that urges Christians to cultivate historic Christian practices, believing that if we do things over and over, Christian practices will eventually become our intuitive way of life.

A growing number of people seek a version of Christian faith that is less interested in institutions and more focused on relationship, community, and mission. These groups sometimes give relatively little formal attention to the Apostles' Affirmation per se, but they tend to share its faith.

Direct Communication from God

Many Christians in the contemporary era believe that God directly communicates in modes already discussed. Pentecostals, for instance, believe that they have a direct experience of the Holy Spirit, especially in tongues, in visions, and in messages that are as straightforward as an article in the newspaper. Pentecostal churches typically believe that God's contemporary messages are consistent with Scripture. Indeed, messages that go against the Bible may be declared inauthentic.

Experience

Some Christians today continue the emphases of natural theology discussed in the previous chapter. Many Christians are inspired to think of God by the splendor or interrelatedness of nature. Echoing natural theology and wisdom, but going a step farther, some Christians believe they can apprehend God through experience. They surmise that since God is always present, we can become aware of God's presence and leading in any moment. Some such people believe that God speaks through contemporary leaders such as Martin Luther King Jr. Some people believe that by engaging in meditative practices, or by otherwise becoming open to God, the thoughts and feelings that come to them are from God. I have an acquaintance, for instance, who, struggling with how to understand an ethical issue, lay down under a tree and attempted to become open to God. This person concluded that the feeling of peace that accompanied a certain perception must have indicated God's approval. Needless to say, the community that follows this way of thinking faces the question of criteria: What gives such a person the confidence that a feeling, or even a verbal statement that may come to mind, is from God?

Scientific Worldview

The scientific worldview became widespread during and after the Enlightenment (beginning in the early eighteenth century). This view holds that a community can accept as true only things that can be verified by the senses. By means of such investigation, scientists identify laws by which the universe operates.[3] Of course, the Bible and traditional Christian doctrine contain stories and ideas that violate scientific laws.

The church today is divided regarding how to relate the Bible, tradition, and contemporary belief with the scientific worldview. Some argue that the Bible is inspired and, therefore, true. The events in the Bible thus took place according to God's supernatural intervention—the opening of the Red Sea during the exodus from Egypt, for instance, took place as reported.

Other Christians note that many stories in the Bible (and some affirmations of Christian tradition) violate the scientific worldview. They cannot be factually verified. Indeed, such texts reflect prescientific worldviews and are expressed in the language and imagery that were meaningful in their original contexts. While the surface level of a text or doctrine may not seem plausible according to the scientific worldview, the interpreter can often identify a deeper purpose of the text that does not depend on the scientific accuracy of the text. For example, while the exodus may not have taken place exactly as described, the text shows that God intends to liberate people from slavery.

In recent years, a Christian movement has argued that the church does not need to concern itself with the ways in which the Bible or beliefs do not satisfy scientific criteria. Indeed, to use scientific criteria to verify the Bible is to let a source outside the Christian house become the source of authority for those within the Christian community.

Instead, we should view the Bible as lifelike material that, similar to great novels, can guide us in life even if specific details cannot be factually verified. For example, the story of the exodus shows that God seeks to open the Red Seas that block our paths to freedom.

Popular Religious Expressions

A lot of people pick up beliefs from popular religious expressions such as the ones that I mentioned at the beginning of the chapter—preachers in the media, local beliefs, or a coffee klatch. You may be driving down the highway and get hooked into a sermon being broadcast on the radio. People in your area may have latched onto a particular set of Bible verses that they pass around and around and around: these verses effectively become a Bible within the Bible. Your neighbor who comes over every day for coffee may bring along some religious ideas she picked up: the general body of religious platitudes that are passed from person to person in our culture. Less consciously you may encounter such things as bumper stickers, lapel pins, wall hangings, greeting cards, Aunt Jenny's constant refrain of "Prayer changes things," singing "God Bless America," or the prayer offered at high school commencement.

Sometimes we consciously embrace ideas in popular religious expression. Sometimes, however, they filter into our wells of religious perception apart from our conscious awareness.

Some of these ideas are consistent with the best religious thinking in the Bible and the tradition, and gleaned from natural theology and experience. But some of these ideas do not measure up to the fullness of Christian understanding. I think, for instance, of people who regard their nation as an idol, or who regard the purpose of Christian faith as motivating people to be good capitalists, or who believe that God wills for certain kinds of people to live in poverty. Consequently, we need to become aware of how we are influenced by popular religious expression so we can draw on it when appropriate but can still criticize it when necessary.

QUESTIONS FOR DISCUSSION

1. As you begin this study, what are the leading ideas in your embedded faith?

2. Do you draw on the Bible as you think about your faith? Which attitudes toward the Bible in this chapter do you find most attractive? Why? Which attitudes do you find not so attractive?

3. Do you draw on tradition as you consider what you believe? Think especially about the Apostles' and Nicene Affirmations of Faith and your denomination's statements of faith. If so, what do you find compelling in this material? What do you find not so compelling?

4. Do you draw on the natural world, your own experience, and your ability to reason as you aim to articulate what you take most seriously in the realm of faith? If so, how do you make use of this material? In particular, what do you do when the tradition says one thing, but your experience seems to tell you something else?

5. How do you regard the scientific worldview relating to faith? If you take the scientific worldview into account, how do you do so?

6. Which resources do you find most authoritative? What makes them so?

7. How do you bring the Bible, tradition, experience, and the scientific worldview into dialogue with one another as you seek to name what you believe?

2
God

What we believe about God is basic to what we believe about all other things. Of course, how we conceive God shapes how we understand Jesus Christ, the Holy Spirit, and the church. In addition, what we believe about God informs how we understand ourselves as human beings, how we interpret the purpose of community, how we envision the purpose of nature and the relationship of humankind and nature, and, of course, what we envision as the ultimate destiny of all things. For instance, if we believe in a loving, gracious, generous God, then we will see all of these things in loving, gracious, generous ways. If we think of God as grumpy and legalistic, we will think of Christ and the Holy Spirit similarly, and we may also become grumpy and legalistic.

The discussion of what we believe about God has two closely related dimensions—God's character and power.[1] God's character refers to what God is like in God's own being.[2] Some readers will be surprised that when speaking of God's power, we have in mind not only the ways that God chooses to use power, but also the extent of God's power. The latter issue arises in a significant way mainly in the contemporary era.

GOD IN THE WORLD OF THE BIBLE

Most sections of this book set out different conceptions of the subject at hand. This section, however, departs from that format. While the Bible contains different nuances in its understandings of God, it does not contain radically different pictures. I report the main lines of an overarching biblical picture of God and note exceptions to that viewpoint.[3]

God as a Personal Being

God is typically pictured in the Bible as a personal being. That is, God is often portrayed as being a distinct entity, with purpose and power. At one level, to oversimplify, we can often think of God in the Bible as a supersize person. God speaks and acts much like a human being, but with hugely greater force. At another level, we need to be careful not to reduce biblical portrayal(s) of God to the image of a supersize person. Biblical writers often speak figuratively of God, using human characteristics. For example, the Chronicler says that "the hand of God was also on Judah to give them one heart" (2 Chr. 30:12). The passage does not literally mean that God has a physical hand, but refers to God's power at work in the world.

In the contemporary era, many people are concerned about the gender of God. It is important to note that while the Bible typically speaks of God in ways that are associated with males, the Bible also pictures God in language and roles associated with women. For example, the Bible speaks of God not only as king, warrior, and father (e.g., Ps. 10:16; Zeph. 3:17; Matt. 6:9), but also as a mother eagle who stirs the nest (Deut. 32:11) and as a mother who carries Israel on her hip, in the manner of a Jewish mother (Isa. 66:12). God cannot forget Israel, in the same way that a nursing mother cannot forget her child (Isa. 49:15). Wisdom is sometimes personified as a woman (e.g., Prov. 1:20–33). Most scholars think that the use of gender characteristics is figurative: The being of God transcends gender, but writers often use gender-related language to speak figuratively of God.

A Relational God Who Responds to the World

Biblical writers typically portray God as being relational in character. God wants to relate to human beings and to the natural world. Moreover, God feels the pain and joy of the world and responds. God responds to the world in ways that human beings perceive as both positive and negative, as both supporting and judging. As an example of

God's positive and assuring response to the world, note that when the children of Israel in slavery in Egypt cry to God, God is moved by their pain (Exod. 3:7). Few passages in the Bible better capture this sense of God than Exodus 34:6–7, which describes God as "merciful and gracious, slow to anger, and abounding in steadfast love and faithfulness, keeping steadfast love for the thousandth generation, forgiving iniquity and transgression and sin, yet by no means clearing the guilty."

God's Larger Purposes Include God's Corrective Purposes

People in the church today sometimes say that the God of the Bible is a God of love *and* wrath, of mercy *and* judgment, and of promise *and* punishment. Ministers sometimes like to contrast the pastoral (caring) side of God with the prophetic (judging) side. Although such expressions rightly call attention to different aspects, the relationship of the different dimensions needs to be nuanced.

From the perspective of the Bible, God's larger purposes are love, mercy, and promise. Those are God's long-term intentions for the community. The community, however, can frustrate God's larger purposes by violating the guidelines of the covenant. At such times, God seeks to correct the community by judgment or punishment. Condemnation is not an end in itself, but is to awaken the community to corrective behavior so that blessing may return. For example, most of the prophets call the community to repent of attitudes and behaviors—such as idolatry and exploitation of the poor—that get in the way of the possibility of blessing.

When circumstances in a particular setting have degenerated to the point that repentance can no longer bring about an immediate renewal, the community can learn from the experience of judgment and can anticipate regeneration in the long term. For God has promised blessing.

An All-powerful God

By and large, the Bible regards God as all-powerful—that is, nothing happens in the world apart from either God's direct initiative or God's permission. God either prompts things to happen or God allows them to happen by not intervening.

Much of the time, the Bible sees a cause-and-effect relationship between the attitude and behavior of the human community and God's action. In the example just above, the community violated the covenant, which caused God to bring judgment upon them. God often seeks to work through agents who can cooperate with God and facilitate God's purposes (e.g., Moses), but who can sometimes get in the way of God's aims by not cooperating with God (e.g., Pharaoh).

However, the relationship between divine activity and human responsibility can be complicated. Ecclesiastes complains of having followed the covenantal rules (so to speak) but finding that life does not conform to them (Eccl. 2:1–11). This author laments that God acts arbitrarily to influence life negatively.

Most people in the biblical world took comfort in God's awesome power. Believing that God either caused or permitted events gave many ancients a sense of security: no matter what happened (for good or ill), they could rest in the security that God was in control. I have heard many Christians use ideas like this one from Isaiah to achieve a satisfactory intellectual understanding of this situation. "My thoughts are not your thoughts, nor are your ways my ways, says [God]. For as the heavens are higher than the earth, so are my ways higher than your ways and my thoughts than your thoughts" (Isa. 55:8–9). People today sometimes use these verses and others like them to assure themselves that God has reasons that are hidden from us for causing or permitting things to happen.

GOD IN THE HISTORY OF THE CHURCH

In its history after the Bible, many churches used aspects of the biblical picture of God. In addition, some in the church turned to Aristotle to help formulate the idea of God as unmoved mover. These issues prompt us to consider some big words that relate to God. In the early Enlightenment period, some people conceived of God as a watchmaker.

Elements of the Biblical God

Voices in the history of the church continue to lift up the biblical pictures of God. But the Bible is a large book, and we creatures have limited minds. We can hardly absorb and talk about the whole of the Bible's understandings of God. Different voices tend to stress particular aspects of the biblical God while often downplaying (even overlooking) other elements.

Often particular aspects of God are important to particular individuals or communities because of the dynamics of their moment in history. When the world feels threatening, for example, a community may emphasize God as the one who controls history. When a particular moment is shot through with legalism, a church may rediscover the grace—unmerited favor—of God.

When developing a faith of our own, two things are often useful. First, we can identify the aspects of the biblical pictures of God that are most important to us and to our church (or the movement with which we identify). Some churches, for instance, emphasize personal holiness. Second, we should also note the aspects of the biblical portraits of God that we downplay. This latter exercise may help us remember aspects of the larger picture of God that we have forgotten. Indeed, by emphasizing only one trajectory in the biblical picture of God, we can misrepresent God's purposes. For example, congregations that emphasize personal holiness sometimes forget that the biblical call is for communities to manifest corporate holiness.

God as Unmoved Mover

The idea of God as unmoved mover originated in technical philosophical discussion, but continues to appear in popular religious expression. As the church in the first centuries began to be less Jewish and more Greek in its membership and orientation, leaders of the church began to interpret the Christian message in categories of Greek thought. Christian thinkers turned most often to Plato and Aristotle for help. With respect to God, the most important and long-lasting development was interpreting God in the conceptuality of Aristotle's unmoved mover. This viewpoint is sometimes called classical theism.

Aristotle reasons backward from everyday experience to the notion of the unmoved mover. Things in the world move. This movement must be caused by something other than the things themselves. If every single thing that moves was moved by something else, then the chain of movers would be infinite. Yet, since the world is finite, there cannot be an infinite chain of movers. Consequently, one mover must have set in motion the very first movement. This first mover cannot have been moved, but must have been an unmoved mover.

Many Christians began to think of God as an unmoved mover. From this point of view, God is the first mover who causes all things to move (all things to occur). God, then, is ultimately responsible for all things, since God sets all things in motion.

Additional ideas came to be associated with the image of God as unmoved mover. In this world of thought, God is changeless (immutable). Neither the being nor the purposes of God change. Another perception is that neither human beings nor other entities in the world can affect God (God is impassable). Indeed, God does not have feelings (emotions). God is not affected by the world. In short, the changeless God cannot be affected or changed by the world. While the unmoved mover causes things to happen in the world, this God is not actually in relationship with human beings or the world, since relationship (by definition) involves reciprocity.

Christian thinkers who advocated this viewpoint claimed that the language in the Bible that describes God as feeling and as responding to the world did not actually describe God but came from the biblical writers' projecting human characteristics onto God. The technical name for this phenomenon is anthropomorphism.

Over the years, typical churchgoing Christians have seldom thought about the formal philosophical rationale for thinking of God as unmoved mover. Indeed, many Christians do not even know that term. However, at the popular level, many Christians in the history of the church thought of God as such a being. They believed that, as the first cause, God was responsible for all things that happened. Since human beings could not affect God, human beings needed to adjust to God's will, that is, to what God caused.

Though Christians had no hope of changing God's will, many sought to understand it. When they could not see a clear reason for what God caused, they took refuge in the idea that we finite creatures cannot understand the infinite God. Many said things like, "God's reasoning is mysterious. We cannot understand God."

Dissatisfaction with this perception of God caused some Christians to ponder how God might be responsive to the world. I take up the most widely followed response below under the heading "A God Who Works through Natural and Supernatural Means."

The Watchmaker God

In the seventeenth and eighteenth centuries, while trying to rationalize the relationship of believing in God with the Enlightenment, several thinkers (often called "deists") put forward the idea of God as a watchmaker. Like Aristotle, they reasoned from present experience to original cause. The existence of a watch implies the existence of a watchmaker. Consequently, the existence of a world implies the existence of one who made it.

Unlike the God of the Bible or the unmoved mover, however, the watchmaker God did not continue to act directly in the world. To oversimplify, this God created natural laws and set the world in motion. Like the watchmaker, God made the world, wound it, put it in place, and stepped away. The world would continue to run on its own.

Three Big Words: All-Knowing, All-Powerful, Always Present

Christians in the history of the church and into today have often discussed God around three big words. These concepts do not represent a distinct view of God so much as they describe characteristics (attributes) of God. People who hold various viewpoints on God from the world of the Bible into today discuss these notions in relationship to God.

The church has often said that God is all-knowing, all-powerful, and always present. By all-knowing (omniscient), Christians have meant that God knows all things. By all-powerful (omnipotent), Christians meant that God can do anything, anytime, anyplace. By always present (omnipresent), the church has meant that God is always present in every moment of every day and that there is never a moment when God is not with us.

These claims raise questions that the church has debated. I cannot resolve these questions in a few sentences, but I can raise some of them. When we say that God is all-knowing, then what do we make of human freedom? Does God know what everyone is going to think and do before we think and do it? Going further, does God know what is going to happen before it happens? If so, what is the point of struggling through tough decisions? When we say that God is all-powerful, does that mean that God actively causes all things, or does God cause some things while passively permitting others? If God is always present, why does God allow horrible things to happen? Why doesn't God intervene? After pondering such questions, some Christians today question whether God is in fact all-knowing (in the sense just articulated), all-powerful, or always present. For this latter viewpoint, see the heading below, "A God with Unlimited Love but Limited Power."

GOD IN CONTEMPORARY PERSPECTIVES

As I have already indicated, several themes from the previous section carry into the contemporary period. Moreover, today's discussions of God are tied closely to God's purposes, which we take up in chapter 6. Our understanding of the character and power of God informs not only how we understand God's purposes but how we believe God carries out those purposes.

Biblical Pictures of God

Of course, most Christians today say they follow biblical pictures of God. But believers today (as in church history) typically lift up certain themes in the Bible while not attending fully to others. When using the Bible as a resource for thinking about God, it is important to be clear as to which biblical traditions are more and which less important, and what is gained and lost by drawing from (and neglecting) particular biblical emphases.

God the Unmoved Mover

Some Christians today continue to think of God as an unmoved mover, in the way we have previously described. While this view of God provides the security of feeling that everything that happens in life can be traced back to a single hand, it continues to raise the vexing questions posed just above.

The Watchmaker God

A few people in the contemporary setting continue to hold the viewpoint of God as cosmic watchmaker. Such folks think that God established natural law and God relates to the world much as a watchmaker passively looking at the watch on the table.

A God Who Works through Natural and Supernatural Means

In response to the Enlightenment, many Christians intensified the distinction between the natural and the supernatural. In this interpretive scheme, God created the world and set it in motion, much like the watchmaker deity (above): from day to day God is largely removed from the world; for its part, the world operates according to natural law. However, unlike such a watchmaker God, this deity can intervene in the world through supernatural means. God can suspend the laws of nature and acts providentially or judgmentally. In the Bible, for instance, God suspends the laws of nature in order to communicate directly with people and to perform miracles (such as opening the Red Sea, healing the woman with the issue of blood, or raising Jesus from the dead (Exod. 14:1–15:18; Mark 5:25-34; 16:1–6).

This God is all-powerful and, consequently, can put creation on hold while carrying out a specific action. While this God lets the world run largely on its own, God can respond with compassion to the cries of the human family and can condemn idolatry or injustice by sending armies to overrun Israel.

My impression is that many Christians today operate with a rough version of this understanding of how God works. They believe that God is watching over the world, but not directly involved in it unless prayer (or something else) prompts God to intervene and change the course that history is following under the influence of natural law.

This view does have its troubles. The language of natural and supernatural is not found in the Bible in the comprehensive way that it is used in this model. The natural and supernatural God is responsible for all things that happen in the world either through setting up the laws of nature or through intervening or not intervening. What does it say about God when a community beseeches God to act in behalf of a poignant situation and God does not do so?

God and Love, Power, and Justice

As in the case of God's being all-knowing, all-powerful, and all-loving (above), these concepts do not represent a distinct view of God as much as they raise a series of issues that are at the heart of how we conceive of God. The church has often asserted that God is simultaneously completely loving, all-powerful, and altogether just.[4] The church has envisioned God as sitting on a stool with three legs of equal size. If this is the case, then in every situation in human life and in the larger world God loves fully, exerts power in loving ways, and acts justly.

At least on the surface, however, some circumstances seem to deny that these three values are equally expressed. The untimely death of an innocent child, for instance, seems to suggest that God's power is greater than God's love, since God caused the child to die. Where is love or justice in that situation?

As in Christian history, some believers think that the problem is not in God's actions but in our limited perceptions. Since God is all-loving, all-powerful, and all-just, God must have perspectives on situations like the death of the innocent child that we humans do not have. However, Christians in our next category take quite a different view. For them, the legs on the stool on which God sits are not of equal length.

A God with Unlimited Love but Limited Power

The school of thinking called process (or relational) thought posits a very different understanding of God than we have encountered thus far. These thinkers believe that God is made up of two interrelated dimensions—an enduring part and an adaptable part.[5] The enduring part is God's unconditional love for the world. But God adapts specific expressions of love to the concrete situations among human beings and in the world. God always seeks to express unconditional love, but God's actions of love vary according to the possibilities and requirements of each situation. From this perspective, God has unlimited love for each entity in creation—human beings, animals, rocks, and trees. God expresses that love in ways that are appropriate for each new situation.

These thinkers believe that it is impossible to say that God is simultaneously all-loving, all-powerful, and all-just. If God is all-loving and all-just *and* all-powerful, God would have to end suffering. An all-loving God could not permit the continuation of suffering. Therefore, Christians in this house believe that God has limited power. God has more power than any other entity, but God is not all-powerful and cannot do anything God wants at any time. God works in the world through lure, that is, God offers the human family the highest possible experience of love in every situation. God also seeks to work collaboratively with people and with elements of nature. When we cooperate with God, we help God realize God's purposes. When we fail to cooperate with God, we frustrate those purposes.

These possibilities may be limited by circumstances. When circumstances prevent as full a concrete expression of divine love as God would like, God adapts to the things that are possible. For example, an illness may have progressed to the point that it is obviously going to bring about death. God cannot singularly change that situation. However, God is with the dying person so that the sufferer does not die alone, but in the companionship of the infinitely loving God.

By way of full disclosure, I subscribe to this point of view. Still, this God of unlimited love but limited power does face serious questions. One of my friends refers to this deity as a "wimp God," that is, a God who cannot do much alone but must always work with and through others. "What is the point of believing in such a God?" my friend asks. I answer that this perception of God better honors both the core of Christian tradition concerning God's love for the world and our actual experience than any other picture of God known to me. Moreover, it provides a picture of God that is seriously believable.

A Nonpersonal God

Christians have usually thought of God as a personal entity, much like a superperson. A few Christians, however, speak of God in nonpersonal terms. Indeed, some Christians do not envision God as a distinct entity or being. In formal theological circles, Paul Tillich is perhaps the most well-known exponent of this approach, in referring to God as "being itself." For Tillich, God is not a distinct being, but is the very power of being that pervades everything. Tillich conceives of God not as impersonal, but as transpersonal.[6] I have heard other Christians refer to God as the power of love or the power of life or the power of history. Some process thinkers describe God as the power of becoming or the power of life process.

Christians in this stream of thought say that to speak of God as a specific being or as having personality is to confine our perceptions of God to our own imaginations. This school of thought seeks to emphasize that God is always more than we can imagine. At the same time, some Christians find it difficult to speak meaningfully of such a God acting in history. Seminary students often say they initially find it hard to relate in a personal way to God as "being itself." However, over time, many students say they develop a deep and visceral living sense of this God.

God and the Gods

Christianity continues to be the largest single religious group in North America, but the religious scene on this continent is an increasingly pluralistic world. In chapter 9, we take up the relationship of Christianity to other religions. For now, we should note that an important issue in interreligious discussion is how the God of the Bible relates to other deities (and understandings of transcendent reality). Is the God of Christian faith the only deity, so that all other gods are idols? Or are the gods of other religions really just different names for the same ultimate reality?

Such questions are more and more important as North America becomes ever more multicultural, with people of different religions living next door to one another. As noted at the beginning of the chapter, what we believe about God contributes significantly to how we think, feel, and act. This is especially true when it comes to how we relate to other people, especially those whose understandings of religion and ultimate reality differ from ours.

QUESTIONS FOR DISCUSSION

1. Thinking back to the notion of an embedded faith discussed in chapter 1, what is your embedded understanding of God?

2. Prayer is often a litmus test for what a specific theology asks you
   to believe. Here is an exercise to bring some of the different understandings of God in this chapter into view. Suppose a member of your congregation has been in an automobile accident
   and is in critical condition in the hospital. Write a brief prayer
   in behalf of that person from the perspective of the following
   understandings of God:
   a. The unmoved mover
   b. The watchmaker God
   c. The natural/the supernatural God
   d. The God of unlimited love but limited power
3. What qualities are most important to you concerning God's
   character? God's power? God's purposes?
4. In view of the qualities that are most important to you concerning God's character, purpose, and power, which picture(s) of
   God in this chapter do you find most compelling? Why?
5. How would adopting this view of God help you, your community, and the world?
6. What questions do you have about the picture of God that you
   find not so compelling? Why?
7. What are your most important questions and issues concerning
   this less attractive option?
8. How does your developing understanding of God compare and
   contrast with your embedded understanding? What do you gain
   or lose with each notion?

3
Jesus Christ

Jesus Christ is at the heart of the church. The very name "Christian" is derived from Christ, and we call ourselves disciples of Christ. Easter, the most important day in the Christian calendar, celebrates the resurrection of Jesus. Most churches have a cross in the sanctuary. The Sunday service often includes the assurance, "In the name of Jesus Christ, your sins are forgiven." The church is called the body of Christ.

Because of the centrality of Jesus in the church, some Christians are caught off guard to learn that the church has interpreted the nature and work of Christ in different ways. Who was he, and what was his purpose?

A book tracing how people have understood Jesus through the years concluded that we tend to imagine Jesus as having our own values and concerns.[1] One of my students said, "I used to think of Jesus as a suburban member of Kiwanis who plays golf a little under par." This chapter introduces us to the ways that some others have pictured Jesus.

JESUS CHRIST IN THE BIBLE

You might expect the New Testament to picture Jesus in a uniform way. But these foundational writings offer diverse views.[2]

29

Prophet of the End-Time

The most pervasive view of Jesus in the New Testament is as prophet (or agent) of the end-time. Many Jewish people accepted the following outline of history: Eve and Adam lived in the Garden of Eden. But when they ate the forbidden fruit, God cursed the world. God divided history into two ages. The present evil age, in which Satan and the demons had extensive power, was marked by sin, sickness, oppression, hunger, enmity with nature, and death. But God promised to bring a new age, often called the realm of God, that would be an age of forgiveness, health, justice, abundance, peace with nature, and eternal life in a resurrection body. An apocalypse would be the means of transition from the present to this realm. God would welcome the faithful into this realm but consign the unfaithful to punishment. Prior to the apocalypse, suffering would increase as the powers of evil entrenched themselves.

According to Paul, the death and resurrection of Jesus signal that the turning of the ages is at hand. Paul urges readers to live faithfully so they will be prepared for the realm (e.g., 1 Thess. 4:13–5:9; 1 Cor. 15:50–57; 2 Cor. 4:16–5:10; Rom. 8:18–25). Mark, Matthew, and Luke share the view that Jesus was a prophet whose message was that the end-time is at hand (Mark 1:14–15; Matt. 4:17; Luke 4:16–30). The ministry of Jesus embodied the realm in the present. They believed they were living in the end-time and that the apocalypse would be Jesus' return from heaven on the clouds (Mark, chap. 13; Matt. 24:1–44; Luke 21:5–33). The death of Jesus is a part of the suffering of the last days, and the resurrection is the definitive demonstration that the realm is at hand. Most other writings in the New Testament share this perspective.

Welcoming Gentiles in Preparation for the Realm

The Old Testament centers on the God of Israel and on the Jewish people. However, the purpose of Israel's life was to be a conduit through which God would bless Gentiles (e.g., Gen. 12:1–3; Isa. 42:6). At the time of Jesus, many Jewish people thought that fullness of blessing would come to Gentiles only in the realm of God described above.

The original followers of Jesus were Jewish. After the resurrection, many of Jesus' followers believed that Christ made it possible for Gentiles to become a part of the community awaiting the apocalypse. Paul was apostle to the Gentiles (e.g., 1 Thess. 1:10; Rom. 1:1–6). The Gospels see welcoming Gentiles as integral to the mission of the church (Mark 13:10; Matt. 28:16–20; Luke 24:44–49; Acts 1:6–11).

This theme is important to virtually all the readers of this book, because we are Gentiles. Apart from Jesus Christ, we might still be engaging in typical Gentile behavior—worshiping idols and living unjustly and violently.

At the Right Hand of God (God's Agent Ruling the World)

In antiquity the right hand was the hand of power. To be at the right hand was to be vested with authority to carry out the purposes of the one who had that hand. The New Testament refers to Jesus being at the right hand of God, the absolute sovereign (see, e.g., Acts 7:55–56; Rom. 8:34; Col. 3:1; Heb. 1:3; 10:12; 1 Pet. 3:22). As agent of God, Jesus is ruler of all the rulers of the earth.

This image is political and polemical. The early church lived when Caesar claimed to be sovereign. Picturing Jesus at the right hand of God assured believers that Christ is greater than Caesar. They should remain faithful as they await the realm.

While the book of Revelation does not speak of Jesus at the right hand of God, it pictures Jesus as sovereign over Caesar (e.g., Rev. 1:12–17; chap. 5; chaps. 19–20). The designation "Lord" captures this dynamic, for a lord ruled over a specific sphere of life. To call Jesus "Lord" is to assert his sovereignty over all other rulers.[3]

Jesus Reveals God

The Gospel and letters of John presuppose a different picture of the universe and a different understanding of Jesus. The universe is divided into two spheres of experience that are related like two stories of a house. Figuratively speaking, the upper sphere, heaven, is the domain of God and is an experience of life, light, truth, love, and freedom. The lower sphere, the world, is the domain of the devil and is an experience of death, darkness, falsehood, hatred, and slavery. People in the world do not know God.

Jesus is the Word who was with God in heaven (John 1:1–5). Because God loved the world, God sent Jesus down into the world to reveal God (John 3:16–21). The revealer not only points to God but creates the possibility of experiencing heaven in the midst of the world. Even more, Jesus ascended to heaven and opened a path that others can follow, so that after death they can be in heaven (John 3:11–13; 14:1–7; 20:17). In the meantime, Jesus' followers are to live together in love (John 13:31–35; 15:18–16:4; chap. 17).

Many people today like the idea of living in a sphere of existence marked by qualities of heaven. They regard the language of the two-story universe (heaven above/world below) as a figure of speech and not a description of physical reality.

Pioneer Who Leads Many People to Heaven

Hebrews also presupposes a two-story universe. Going further, Hebrews interprets existence from the perspective of a form of Judaism whose goal is to help people go from the lower sphere (world, imperfection, old covenant, earthly sanctuary) to the upper sphere (heaven, perfection, heavenly sanctuary, new covenant, rest).

Jesus is the pioneer who leads many children to heaven (Heb. 2:10–13). Jesus experienced life in the world as a human being, tasting temptation, suffering, and death (see, e.g., Heb. 2:14–18; 4:14–5:10; chap. 7). Hebrews' emphasis is not on the mechanics of Jesus as high priest, sacrifice, and new covenant but is on using this imagery to assure readers that by following Jesus they will complete the journey from the world to heaven.

Died for Us

Over the years, I have often asked Bible-study groups, "What does Jesus do for you?" The most common answer is "Jesus died for us." I think most people have in mind that Jesus died in our place (substitutionary atonement).[4] The New Testament does explain the death of Jesus as a form of atonement (e.g., 1 Pet. 2:24), though not in the fully developed notion of substitutionary atonement (as explained below).[5]

The New Testament interprets the death of Jesus in many different ways, such as: ransom (Mark 10:45); blood of the covenant (Mark 14:24); martyr (Acts 7:51–52); revelation of glory (John 17:1); justification and reconciliation (Rom. 5:9–10); paschal lamb (1 Cor. 5:7);

redemption (Eph. 1:7); victory over the powers (Col. 2:14–15); sacrifice that takes away sin (Heb. 9:23–10:39); and defeat of Satan (Rev. 12:7–12). Of course, each of these images must itself be explained in detail.

The death of Jesus is seldom an end in itself, but is connected with the resurrection. The death and resurrection *together* signal redemption. The abundance of such diverse images suggests that the early church focused less on the religious mechanics of what happened when Jesus died and more on the effect of the death in the context of the resurrection. These events assure us that God loves us and acts in our behalf.

JESUS IN THE HISTORY OF THE CHURCH

The history of the church contains multiple interpretations of Christ. Indeed, certain moments in the history of the church have been defined by conflicts regarding how to understand Jesus Christ.

Jesus Is a Created Being

Christians today sometimes think that the church always assumed that Jesus is God in the flesh, the second person of the Trinity. However, the church did not formally make that decision until the fourth century at the Councils of Nicaea and Constantinople. Prior to that time, the church debated the relationship of Jesus to God, with many Christians holding that Jesus was not God. One form of this way of thinking was called adoptionism—at a certain moment in history God adopted Jesus. Another form of this thought came from one of the most well-known figures in these debates, Arius (ca. 250–336 CE), who held that God and Jesus were not of the same essence (substance) and that God begot (created) Jesus. However, since God created the world through Jesus, Jesus must have existed before the beginning of this world. The later church called this way of thinking a heresy, and used the name Arianism for it.

Although the Council of Nicaea denounced Arius's views, many Christians continued to believe as Arius did. Through the centuries (including today) occasional Christians have held views similar to those of Arius. Indeed, some Christians think that Arius held too high a view of Jesus.

Jesus Is God in the Flesh: The Second Person of the Trinity

Most understandings of Jesus from the history of the church into the present day think of Jesus as God in the flesh (God incarnate), the second person of the Trinity.[6] Although many Christians today refer to this notion as *the* orthodox view, it was not fully formulated and adopted by the church until the Council of Chalcedon in 451. Reflecting the fact that the church had become less Jewish and more Greek, this council formalized an interpretation of Jesus that is Greek in orientation. Along the way, the church rejected other interpretations of Jesus.

This viewpoint holds that Jesus is fully divine and fully human, with these two natures united in one person. Jesus is not two entities (God and a human being) in one body, but is one person with no separation of natures. Jesus had the full knowledge of God while also the knowledge that comes to human beings as a result of living in the world. While Jesus was of the same substance as human beings, Jesus did not sin.

Critics point out that this fully developed view is not found explicitly in the Bible. Moreover, Christians often fixate more on one aspect of Jesus than another. It raises questions that sometimes distract Christians. For example, someone asked, "If Jesus is God, why did Jesus pray?"

Jesus the Victor over Evil

The notion of Christ as victor is similar to that of Jesus as end-time prophet and of Jesus at the right hand of God (discussed above). The heart of this approach is that through Christ God wins the victory over the power of Satan, sin, and death.

In the early centuries of the first millennium, some Christians gave this viewpoint an interesting twist: Satan had ruled humankind since the fall. God offered the death of Jesus to Satan as a ransom paid to Satan for the release of the world. God tricked Satan, however, by offering a victim who was God incognito and who could sneak up on Satan. Some Christians charge that this view compromises the sovereignty of God and ends in a hopeless dualism in which God has to satisfy the demands of the devil.

Although the idea of God's outwitting Satan largely disappeared from the church, aspects of this theory (Christ the victor) appear to the present day. There are similarities between this theory and some contemporary pictures of Christ.

Jesus' Death Makes Substitutionary Atonement (Anselm)

As mentioned above, substitutionary atonement is a popular understanding of the work of Christ. Many Christians today who cannot explain this approach in detail identify with its general lines.

Associated with Anselm (1033–1109), this view holds that God is sovereign. While humankind owes God honor, sin makes it impossible for us to render the honor that God is due. God, then, has two choices: (1) God can punish humankind for its failure, or (2) God can accept a substutionary payment. With respect to the second option, since human beings owe a debt to God, the substitution can be made only by a human being, but typical human beings are incapable of making reparation. However, Christ can make satisfaction, since Christ is both God and human. Christ substitutes for us, doing what we could not do.[7] Christ's substitution propitiates God, that is, turns away God's wrath.

This approach is sometimes called the objective approach because it changes the objective (actual) relationship between God and humankind. Apart from Christ, human beings are actually alienated from God and subject to wrath. Christ changes that situation.

This view stresses the priority of God's grace (unmerited favor) in effecting salvation. Human beings can do nothing other than trust in what Christ has done. In our own time, however, some people dislike this theory because it pictures God as requiring violence in order to be satisfied. Proponents of the theory point out that since Christ is God, God receives the violence into God's own self.

Jesus' Death Affects Humankind (Abelard)

Whereas substitutionary atonement focuses on satisfying God's requirements for justice, a Christian named Peter Abelard (1079–1144 CE) shifted the emphasis to the effect of the death of Christ on the believer. God always loves human beings. However, the human heart, hardened by sin, does not know God and fears God. In contrast to substitutionary atonement, the human being does not owe God repayment of a debt, but simply does not respond appropriately to the love of God. The work of Christ does not change God's attitude to humankind, but awakens humankind to God's love for us. Christ alerts human beings to God's love for them.

This approach is sometimes called the subjective approach because it seeks to change the human being's subjective (changeable) impression of God. Jesus invites people to perceive what God is already doing for them.

Quite a number of Christians today find this view attractive. Critics, however, charge that it shifts the focus from God's grace to human response, and can easily drift into works-righteousness, that is, the idea that human beings must perform certain works to merit God's love. Proponents of this view reply that we cannot awaken our own loving response to God on our own. Christ graciously does that.

Jesus Is the Great Example

Although Christ as example is a spin-off from Christ affecting humankind (Abelard), it has had a far-reaching life of its own. In this popular way of thinking, Christ provides the model for how God relates to human beings and how human beings should relate to one another. Christ shows us what we must do if we are to receive God's love and live faithfully.

I know Christians who say that we are saved *through* following Christ. Salvation, then, results from obedience. If we do not follow Christ's example, we do not receive God's love and cannot be saved. This approach is works-righteousness.

Jesus as a Figure of History

Beginning in the late 1700s, some Christians viewed the Bible through the lens of the Enlightenment understanding of history and myth. History consists of facts that actually can be verified by scientific methods. Myth refers to stories that did not actually happen but that ancient people told to explain their feelings about the world. According to the mythic worldview, for instance, the world was inhabited by invisible beings who could cause events to take place that violated natural law.

Some Christians sought to distinguish between Jesus as a figure in history and Jesus as the church mythically interpreted him. These folks regarded the virgin birth, the miracles, and the resurrection as myth. Thomas Jefferson, for instance, physically snipped the stories containing miraculous elements out of his copy of the New Testament.

Some Christians continue to distinguish between history and myth. This effort yields a picture of Jesus that is at home in the Enlightenment worldview, but is removed from the living experience of Christ at the center of the faith of the church.

Jesus Opposes Judaism

Although not a distinct interpretation of Jesus, the notion that Jesus opposed Judaism has been a staple in much Christian thought and appeared in many of the viewpoints in the history of the church and even in our contemporary era. According to this perception, Jesus was opposed to Judaism because it was legalist, rigid, substituted empty ceremony for ethical living, lacked compassion, and stood for salvation by works. This attitude fed anti-Judaism (prejudice against Jewish people and practices) and anti-Semitism (systematic racial hatred against the Jewish people as a whole), and contributed not only to the Inquisition, but ultimately to the Holocaust, with the murder of six million European Jews by Nazi Germany.

Scholars today conclude that this picture of Judaism is a misunderstanding. Judaism was a religion of grace, with love for God and neighbor, and called for ethical living. Jesus himself participated fully in Judaism. However, after his death and resurrection some of his followers came into conflict with some Jewish people regarding whether Gentiles could be admitted to the eschatological community without being fully initiated into Judaism. To justify their position, the Gospel writers intensified the picture of Jesus in conflict with Jewish leaders. The Gospel writers thrust their conflict with Jewish leaders in their own day back into the story of Jesus.

JESUS IN THE CONTEMPORARY CHURCH

The contemporary church reweaves several threads from our previous sections in indicating the significance of Jesus Christ. Several motifs from these different perspectives intertwine with one another.

Jesus Is the Human Face of God (Second Person of the Trinity)

Many Christians in our contemporary era view Jesus as the second person of the Trinity. In today's church, however, the emphasis is often on Jesus as the human face of God. The incarnation assures people that

God understands the human situation today. Since God has been one of us, we know that God empathizes with us.

Substitutionary Atonement

Many Christians today continue to view the work of Jesus as substitutionary atonement. I hear people say they are drawn to this view in order (a) to be saved from punishment, (b) to experience the joy of knowing their debt is paid, and (c) to add to God's joy as sinners come to embrace what God has done for them through Christ.

Jesus Will Come Again

This viewpoint focuses on the second coming as the center of the meaning of Christ. Some expressions of this perspective share similarities with Christ as end-time prophet, except that they believe that the early twenty-first century (or some era soon to come) is the end. Indeed, such folk often regard the present as a time of suffering that will soon end. Those who regard the return of Christ as the central tenet of what they believe about Christ usually also regard the most important tasks of the church to be to alert people to the imminence of that return and to help people prepare for it.

Jesus Is Agent of the Present and Coming Realm

Quite a few Christians are drawn to the idea that Christ is God's agent in manifesting God's realm in the present, while recognizing that the world awaits the final and full coming of this realm. This viewpoint is a spin on Christ as end-time prophet and is often closely related to Christ the liberator (immediately below). Many people who follow this line of thought focus on Christ as a living presence, who manifests the realm in the present through personal and communal experiences and through social moments. Christians in this world of thought often say that the realm is both present and coming, already and not yet.

The death of Christ is often interpreted as the result of those who oppose the realm. The death of Christ was less salvific than it was a sign of how savagely the powers of evil opposed Christ in antiquity and oppose Jesus' followers today. Some Christians downplay the future aspect and concentrate almost solely on the present.

Jesus Is the Liberator

Christ as liberator is another spin on the motifs of Christ as seated at the right hand of God, Christ as agent of God's realm, and Christ as victor. This interpretation regards the primary problem in the world as oppression, in matters such as race and ethnicity, gender, age, social class, national home, colonial occupation, gender orientation, and religious affiliation. Christ liberates people from all forms of oppression. For example, Christ liberates African Americans from racism. Christ frees women from sexism.

Within the general paradigm of Christ as liberator, some Christians envision Christ in terms of their own group. Thus, for instance, we encounter the African American Christ and the feminist Christ. Indeed, some women interpret Christ through the biblical notion of wisdom, because the Bible sometimes personifies wisdom as a woman.

Some Christians who follow this lead believe that the liberating work of Christ may take place through violence—for example, the liberation of oppressed people in Africa or Latin America must sometimes come about through armed revolt. Unimaginable numbers of people are repressed, often in unimaginable ways. The prospect of Christ as liberator is potent. But can all distortions in humankind and nature (and all the work of Christ) be explained as oppression and liberation?

Jesus Is Leader of Nonviolent Resistance

This notion of Christ shares important characteristics with the three preceding models in that it pictures Christ as seeking a world of justice for all. A primary work of Christ here is to lead in nonviolent resistance against the principalities and powers that deform life. The hope is that nonviolence will inspire change. An obvious issue for this way of interpreting Christ is the limits of nonviolence. When suffering caused by social forces seems unlikely to end, how long does a community continue practicing nonviolence?

Jesus Is Living Presence: Friend Who Is Always with Us

Over the past several years, my spouse has served as interim minister in many congregations of the Christian Church (Disciples of Christ) in Indiana. She reports that the most common perception of Jesus in these communities is the great friend who is always with us. Christ is a living presence whom people feel in seasons of distress and grief, who walks with us along life's narrow ways, and who magnifies our joy. Although many people who speak of Jesus as friend think of Jesus as the human face of God, the technical aspects of this perception are secondary to the experience of Jesus as friend.

A lot of people have made their way through illness, divorce, death, and other situations because they felt Jesus' support. But how does Jesus relate to circumstances in which people need not to be reassured but to be confronted with their need to change?

Jesus Is Symbol of God

A symbol is something present that stands for something that is not this symbol. A symbol is finite, and therefore never fully able to make present that which it represents. Nevertheless, it can help human beings perceive what it symbolizes. As a human being, Jesus was a symbol of God in that Jesus' life and ministry made God's rule present. The biblical stories and church's affirmations about Jesus function symbolically, that is, they make God's rule present. Consequently, when we encounter Jesus through the Bible, through preaching and teaching, through the sacraments, and through encounters with other people we become aware of (and are touched by) God's realm.

Some Christians who follow the idea of God as unlimited in love but limited in power regard Jesus-as-symbol as a lure toward God's purposes. Indeed, Jesus-as-lure is one way that God works in the world. When we respond positively to the lure represented in Jesus, we cooperate with God and experience as much of God's realm as our circumstances permit.

Jesus as Sage and Poet

Over the last twenty years, the Jesus Seminar has received a lot of publicity. This group, comprised of biblical scholars, is among the contemporary heirs to the quest to identify Jesus as a figure of history (above). The members of the Jesus Seminar seek to leave behind the religion *about* Jesus and to return to the religion *of* Jesus.

The seminar concludes that Jesus did not believe in the apocalyptic end of history or in hell as a place of punishment, that he did not perform miracles or rise from the dead. Instead, Jesus was an itinerant sage who encouraged his followers toward the wisdom to recognize that God's realm was already present. Although this principle was often unseen by the casual eye, it reversed many conventional assumptions. Jesus demonstrated this rule by eating with sinners and engaging in other behaviors that (like many of his sayings) turned traditional expectations upside down. This Jesus preached and taught in figures of speech (especially parables and pithy sayings). Jesus was in conflict with the Jewish establishment and with other conventional groups. For Jesus, God was a loving parent.

This Jesus reflects the values of many progressive folk in early twenty-first-century circles. However, this wisdom teacher is far removed from the living Christ that many people continue to experience. Indeed, this Jesus is much like the Great Example (in the preceding section). Moreover, some scholars question whether we have the sources and the methods to create such a comprehensive picture of Jesus as a figure in history.

Jesus Is Present through the Community of the Church

Folks in this group recognize that Christ is present in many ways, but their primary experience of Christ is through the community of the church. They encounter the risen Jesus in relationships with individuals, when gathering with small groups, through participating in worship, and while working with one another in mission. For such believers, the church is, indeed, the body of Christ.

QUESTIONS FOR DISCUSSION

1. Recalling the notion of embedded faith in chapter 1, what is your embedded understanding of Jesus Christ? You might think of a moment in life when Jesus has been most important to you. Which image(s) of Jesus in this chapter (or others) best help interpret that experience?

2. The church has often affirmed that Jesus is both fully divine and fully human. How important is it for you to envision Jesus in this way? If so, why is it important? What do you gain with this way of understanding? What, if anything, do you think people lose if they do not believe that Jesus is fully human and fully divine? If you do not think it is important to think of Jesus as fully divine and fully human, what do you gain with that viewpoint? What, if anything, do you think people lose when they do think of Jesus as fully divine and fully human?

3. The work of Christ is, in part, to respond to a need in the life of the world. Each image of Jesus in this chapter responds to a particular need in human life. For example, Christ the liberator responds to the condition of oppression and the need for liberation. What are the greatest needs in your life and in the life of the world? Which image(s) of Jesus respond to those needs?

4. The work of Christ is also, in part, to help individuals and communities manifest God's purposes most fully. Christ as agent of the realm, for instance, seeks to help people to recognize the realm of God and to live in its fullness. From this point of view, which picture(s) of Jesus Christ in this chapter do you find most compelling? What makes it or them compelling? How do those pictures help you?

5. What questions do you have about the picture(s) of Jesus Christ you have just identified as compelling?

6. Which images of Jesus in this chapter are not compelling to you? Indeed, do you find some of these images unattractive? Why do you not like these images?

7. How does your developing understanding of Jesus Christ compare and contrast with your embedded understanding? What do you gain and lose with each notion?

4

The Holy Spirit

Compared to God and Jesus Christ, the Holy Spirit has had a checkered relationship with the church. Some churches give the Holy Spirit so little attention that you would hardly know the Spirit exists. A few churches place so much emphasis on the Holy Spirit that I want to stand up and say, "Hey, remember God? Remember Jesus?" I find in Bible-study groups that a number of laypeople have a foggy view of the Spirit and its work. "Just what is the Spirit anyway? How can I tell the Spirit is around?"

An older way of speaking about the Spirit adds to this uncertainty. When I was growing up, people typically referred to the Spirit as the Holy Ghost. This image often prompted people to imagine the Spirit as a ghost, that is, as a shadowy figure much like the ghosts that we see at Halloween. Even though I knew from the few references to the Spirit in our church that we were supposed to have a positive (holy!) view of the Spirit, this popular image of the Spirit as ghost left dimensions of uncertainty, even spookiness in my mental associations with the Holy Spirit. Over the years I have found that many people in my generation (Boomers) share this hesitation.

THE HOLY SPIRIT IN THE BIBLE

The English word *spirit* in both Hebrew and Greek can also mean breath or wind. In this basic usage, the word *spirit* does not refer to the Holy Spirit, but to the act of breathing or the blowing of the wind. By analogy, biblical writers use the word *spirit* to speak of the Holy Spirit to indicate that it is as important as breath, and it has power and mobility like the wind. In the Bible, the Spirit is one of God's closest agents.[1]

Preserving Chaos

Christians sometimes think that God created the world out of nothing. According to Genesis 1:1–2, however, chaos ("formless void," "face of the deep") existed before God began to create. But "a wind from God swept over the face of the waters," thus preserving the chaos from self-destruction. The chaos contained incredible energy, but the energy was wild, frenetic, and even destructive. God fashioned the world out of the chaos, that is, God took the energy and gave it shape and focus (Gen. 1:3–2:4). This notion is suggestive for understanding a work of the Spirit today: God seeks to preserve the energy that is present in chaos in the hope of turning that energy in a creative direction.

Assisting with Creation

An important clue to the relationship of the Spirit and God is given in Psalm 33:6 when the writer says, "By the word of [God] the heavens were made, and all their host by the breath of [God's] mouth." The Word and the breath (Spirit) are parallel in function. They are not the same as God, but are agents used by God.

Sustaining Creation

According to some biblical writers, God sustains the world through the Spirit. Psalms describes God providing food for all the creatures that God has made. Yet, "When you [God] hide your face, they [created beings] are dismayed; when you take away their breath [Spirit], they die" (Ps. 104:29). The Spirit constantly maintains life in the created world. Although the Spirit may be more manifest at certain times (see below), the Spirit is always at work keeping people and the cosmos alive.

Re-creating Community

Human communities sometimes lose their created purpose and degenerate into chaos. For instance, when Israel forsook the covenant by worshiping idols, exploiting the poor, and seeking security in violence, God cursed the community and reduced their life to chaos. The community's unfaithfulness caused nature to revert to chaos. God sends the Spirit to help re-create both the human community and the natural world. Isaiah says that God will pour out the Spirit on the desolate community with an effect similar to pouring water on thirsty land. "They shall spring up like . . . willows by flowing streams" (Isa. 44:4; cf. 32:14–20). This theme assures communities that though personal and social situations may drift into chaos, as God created originally through the Spirit, God re-created in Israel, and can re-create today.

Animating Wisdom

Although the wisdom tradition has relatively less interest in the Spirit than other Jewish groups in the Bible, this tradition sometimes notes that the Spirit animates both people who are wise and wisdom itself. For instance, the Wisdom of Solomon, a book found in the Apocrypha, says explicitly, "For your immortal spirit is in all things," with the result that as people make their way through life, little by little, God corrects people (Wis. 12:1–2).

Inspiring People for Leadership

The Spirit inspires people for particular acts of ministry. The judges, for instance, are touched by the Spirit at crucial moments (Judg. 3:10; 11:29; 14:6). The book of Isaiah describes the ideal ruler of Israel as inspired by the Spirit (e.g., Isa. 11:12; 42:6; 61:1). The Spirit empowers Ezekiel and the community as a whole toward justice (e.g., Ezek. 36:26–27; 37:1–14). In Joel, the Spirit overcomes distinctions between male and female, young and old, slave and free (Joel 2:28–32).

The baptism of Jesus confirms that Jesus was directed by the Spirit (Mark 1:9–11; Matt. 3:13–17; Luke 3:21–22; John 1:29–34). The Spirit plays a prominent role in the book of Acts, creating the church

as a community in the vision of Joel, and empowering the ministry
of Paul and the Gentile mission (Acts 2:1–21; 4:8; 6:5; 9:17; 10:19;
13:2; etc.). The Spirit inspired both Paul's preaching and the response
of those who welcomed his message (1 Thess. 1:4–7; Rom. 1:4). For
Paul, the Spirit provides the community with many different gifts that
make it possible for the community to carry out its mission (1 Cor. 12;
cf. Eph. 4). The Spirit gave the prophet John the vision of the book of
Revelation (Rev. 1:10).

Filling People with Ecstasy

The Spirit sometimes filled people with ecstasy, that is, with a high-
voltage religious emotion such as like speaking in tongues. God took
some of the Spirit that was on Moses and put it on the elders of Israel
and they prophesied—in other words, they manifested religious ecstasy
(Num. 11:24–25). On the day of Pentecost the Spirit filled the house
where the disciples were waiting and caused them to speak in the many
languages represented among people from the many different nations
who were present, and thereby created one real *community* out of the
different nations (Acts 2:1–13; contrast Gen. 11:1–19). At Corinth,
many in the congregation spoke in glossolalia (unknown tongues). Paul
acknowledges the validity of tongues, but cautions that this gift is to
be used for the upbuilding of the community (1 Cor. 14:26–33a). In
particular, religious ecstasy is to lead people to love (1 Cor. 13). How
do we recognize when someone is filled with the Spirit? When a person
is inspired by the Spirit, that person cooperates with God's desires for
love and justice.

Sign of the End-Time

Some writers in the New Testament believed that the outpouring of
the Spirit would be a sign of the end-time as well as a source of support
for the community as it suffered in the last days. Paul describes the
Spirit as the first fruits of the coming of the realm (Rom. 8:23; 2 Cor.
1:21–22; 5:5; cf. Acts 2:17–21). During the end-time, the Spirit is a
source of strength, even interpreting our groans (Rom. 8:26–27).

Continuing Presence of Jesus with the Community

Although Luke-Acts and the gospel and letters of John differ in many ways, they share the viewpoint that, after Jesus ascends to heaven the Spirit continues the ministry of Jesus in the church. In Luke-Acts, the Holy Spirit enables the church to continue to do what Jesus did: preach, teach, heal, and even raise the dead. The Johannine Jesus says, "I will ask [God, who] will give you another Advocate, to be with you forever." This Advocate (the Spirit) abides with the community in the same way that Jesus abides with the community and with God (John 14:16, 26; 15:26; 16:7).

People Can Turn Away from the Spirit

Several of the biblical writers acknowledge that the human will often plays a role in responding to the Holy Spirit. People can cooperate with the Spirit or resist. For example, Isaiah declares that the community rebelled against God in the wilderness and grieved the Holy Spirit (Isa. 63:10; cf. Eph. 4:30). Paul notes that people can walk with or against the Spirit (Rom. 8:1–17; Gal. 5:16–26).

THE HOLY SPIRIT IN THE HISTORY OF THE CHURCH

The history of the church contains many interpretations of the Holy Spirit. I report a cross section of viewpoints to illustrate the centers of gravity in interpretations.

The Spirit Supersedes Sacred Tradition (Montanus)

Montanus (second century CE) believed not only that God's revelation did not end with the apostles but that Montanus himself was an oracle of continuing revelation and that the words of the Spirit through him were more authoritative than the words of sacred tradition. Montanus received his messages by falling into religious ecstasy. Eventually many churches declared that Montanus was a false prophet.

God Created the Spirit (Macedonianism, Semi-Arianism).

A person named Macedonius (fourth century CE) taught that Jesus was not of the *same* substance as God, but was of *similar* substance. Macedonius also taught that the Holy Spirit was not eternal with God but that God created the Spirit and operated the Spirit through Jesus. The movement, known as Macedonianism, was similar to a phenomenon called Semi-Arianism. This latter group received their name from Arius, who taught that Jesus was not God but was created by God. The Semi-Arians believed that Jesus was God, but they insisted that the Holy Spirit was not God. They believed that the Spirit was a finite entity who operated in the world much like an angel.

The Church in the West: Third Person of the Trinity—The Lord, the Giver of Life, Who Proceeds from the Father and the Son

The councils of Nicaea (325 CE) and Constantinople (381 CE) and Chalcedon (451 CE) formulated an understanding of the Holy Spirit that most Christians considered normative in those days and that is still considered normative by many churches today. These councils decided that the Holy Spirit is the third person of the Trinity, that is, the Holy Spirit is God along with Jesus. These councils interpreted the Spirit as being of the same substance with God and Jesus, and not an agent that God created. For these councils the Holy Spirit is the active power of the Godhead at work in the world.

These issues may seem technical and obscure to many Christians today. But, as we explore more fully in chapter 5 (in connection with the Trinity), differences of opinion led to separation of the churches in the West (the churches that became the Roman Catholic Church and the Protestant churches) from those in the East (the group that became the Orthodox churches—Eastern, Greek, Russian, Coptic, etc.).

The Nicene Affirmation of Faith uses the provocative phrase "the Lord, the giver of life" (Ecumenical Version) to describe the Spirit. The phrase "giver of life" emphasizes that the Spirit is means of creation and re-creation. As God created the world, so God can create through the presence of the Spirit.

Source of Visions

As in the world of the Bible, some people in the history of the church believed that the Spirit came directly to them. The mystics, in particular, received visions from the Spirit. The mystic often becomes open to receiving a visitation from the Spirit as a result of a plan to do so, but sometimes in spontaneous response to impulses in the moment. The mystic enters into a state of openness, sometimes ecstatic. The Spirit communicates directly with the mystic in words or visions. For example, the female mystic Julian of Norwich (1342–after 1416) received a vision of hell beyond which was an even greater reality: God's love that finally overcomes the limitations of hell. Julian thus anticipated universal salvation—the belief that ultimately God will save everyone. She also spoke of God and Jesus in the language of motherhood. Of course, this perspective raises the question of how to distinguish between a mystical experience that comes from the Holy Spirit and one that may result from lesser sources.

The Great Awakener

For some Christians the notion of the Holy Spirit as great awakener is a singular role, but for some it is linked to the Spirit as sanctifier (below). The most dramatic instances of the Spirit as awakener in North America are associated with the first and second great religious awakenings (in, respectively, the 1730s-1740s and the 1790s-1840s), and some speak of third and fourth awakenings (1880s-1890s, 1960s-1970s). As the name implies, people believed that the Holy Spirit brought about a personal awakening of the individual to God. Conversion was the most important aspect of awakening. The Holy Spirit would infuse the heart and mind of the individual with awareness of grace, so that the individual would respond with love for God and other people. Many Christians associated with the awakenings thought that the Spirit would bring about this awareness in a relatively brief and intense time. Those awakened sometimes gave demonstrations of being touched by the Spirit, as with singing, groaning, or reports of dreams.

The Sanctifier (Leading People in the Holy Life)

Going beyond awakening, John Wesley (1703–1791) believed that the Holy Spirit effects sanctification, that is, helps people grow toward the holy life. In Greek, sanctification means to become holy. The Holy Spirit sanctifies, that is, empowers people toward holy living, which means living in the way God wants. The heart of holiness is living in the way of love for God and also for others. Some churches have stressed personal holiness, while some holiness churches have been involved in social reform (e.g., abolition of slavery, temperance, prison reform, suffrage). Wesleyans envision sanctification not as a single moment but as an ongoing process: the heart becomes ever more attuned to God's purposes for love; the holy believer can avoid many conscious sins, but can never achieve a sinless life. The Methodist churches, the Wesleyan and Holiness churches, as well as some Pentecostals continue to share elements of this perspective.

THE HOLY SPIRIT IN THE CONTEMPORARY CHURCH

During much of the twentieth century, the long-established churches gave little attention to the Holy Spirit. Indeed, the Spirit was described as the neglected child of Christian doctrine. Today, however, the long-established churches show much more interest in the Holy Spirit, prompted by the presence of Pentecostalism, by a rediscovery of emphasis on the Trinity, and by increased attention to experiential elements of religion. The two basic ways of understanding the Spirit are as the third person of the Trinity and as agent of God. Viewpoints may overlap, however, in connection with particular emphases.

The Third Person of the Trinity

For many Christians today, the Holy Spirit is the third person of the Trinity, as described in the preceding section. My impression is that few laypeople in churches in the West are deeply engrossed by the question of whether the Holy Spirit proceeds from God and Jesus (West) or if the Spirit proceeds from God and rests in Jesus (East). Most people appear to view the Holy Spirit in more functional terms as God at work. This understanding of the Spirit emphasizes that *God* is present and working.

Agent of God

Christians who do not endorse the doctrine of the Trinity view the Holy Spirit as an agent or servant of God, in ways that resemble the biblical writers and those who believe that God created the Spirit (such as the Macedonians and Semi-Arians). While the Spirit is God's agent or representative, the Spirit in this view is not part of the Godhead.

Many people who regard the Holy Spirit as agent of God view the work of the Spirit as continuing the work attributed to the Spirit in the Bible (above): attempting to preserve chaos, sustain creation, re-create the lives of individuals and communities, move the world toward justice, inspire people's leadership, and move people with deep feeling.

In functional terms, the immediate *work* of the Holy Spirit as third person of the Trinity and as agent of God are very similar. The difference in these two perspectives is that those who regard the Spirit as an agent of God believe that they stand on more biblical ground (as in our above discussion).

Working through Social Process

The notion that the Holy Spirit works through social process began in the history of the church and is widely held in progressive religious circles today. For many Christians the work of the Holy Spirit takes place in social life rather than through special events, as well as in the Spirit's work with individuals. Reacting against the great awakenings (above), with their insistence that the Holy Spirit effects dramatic moments of conversion, Horace Bushnell (1802–1876) contended instead that children should be nurtured in the home in the way of Christ so that they would grow up with the gospel imprint. The Holy Spirit works through the parents and the experiences of the child in the Christian household.

This way of thinking can be extended to other aspects of life. In every situation, the Spirit is at work to help people experience and respond to God's purposes of love and justice. For example, at the time of death, the Spirit is present through the community that surrounds the bereaved. People can become conscious of the Spirit by reading the Bible and by gathering around the loaf and the cup. The Spirit is at work through social movements that seek to end racism and sexism and to create a world of love, justice, and peace.[2] When we join such movements, we respond to the leading of the Spirit.

Some Christians believe that the Holy Spirit is universally present among all peoples, urging all toward love, peace, justice, and abundance. People may not name the Holy Spirit as such. They may not recognize the Spirit, indeed they may not even know about the Spirit, but the Spirit is still at work. An important work of the church is to try to discern the leading of the Spirit as distinguished from that of other spirits.

The Gift of the Spirit a Second Work of Grace: The Pentecostal Experience of the Spirit

The contemporary Pentecostal movement began a little over a hundred years ago. Many Pentecostals regard justification (being made right with God) as a first work of grace that, for fullness of Christian experience, should be followed by a second work of grace—being filled with the Holy Spirit.[3] The infilling, sometimes known as the baptism of the Holy Spirit, can be quite dramatic and can take place at the same time as water baptism (which assures persons of justification) or at a different time and place.

Ordinarily, a believer filled by the Spirit speaks in tongues. Some Pentecostals contend, however, that tongues and other dramatic evidences of the Spirit are not required for believers to be confident that they are filled with the Spirit. The baptism of the Spirit has a double purpose: (1) it assures believers that they are filled with the Spirit; and (2) it also empowers for mission.

Some Christians reject the idea that the Spirit works in such dramatic ways. Indeed, a movement called Cessationism argues that when the apostolic age ended, so did tongues and similar gifts.

The Feminine Dimension of the Divine

A growing body of Christians sees the Holy Spirit expressing a feminine dimension in the Godhead. Proponents of this idea point to passages in the Bible that speak of the work of the Spirit in a feminine way. For example, the Wisdom of Solomon says that wisdom holds all things together; for the author of Solomon, wisdom is synonymous with the

Spirit (Wis. 1:7; cf. 7:21–8:1; 9:17). Occasional leaders of the church spoke of the Holy Spirit in feminine language, even calling the Holy Spirit Mother.

The feminine image of the Spirit affirms women's experience and represents the image of God as truly male and female (as implied in Gen. 1:26–27). Since human beings often take the social roles of their deity as models for their own social roles, having a feminine presence in the Godhead implies the equality of women and men. This notion also stresses the importance of using women's experience as a lens for interpreting the nature and work of God.

Continuing Voice of God

As we noted in chapter 1, many Christians believe that God continues to speak, and some people today believe they have come to understand aspects of God and of God's purposes that are quite different from—and more accurate than—earlier notions. Some Christians attribute such newly found perceptions to the Holy Spirit. Indeed some believers, like Montanus, believe that the word of the Spirit received today takes precedence over the Bible and the voice of Christian tradition.

QUESTIONS FOR DISCUSSION

1. Recalling the notion of embedded faith in chapter 1, what is your embedded understanding of the Holy Spirit?
2. How has this chapter prompted fresh thoughts about the Holy Spirit, or new images, or questions that you have not previously asked?
3. The church has often affirmed that the Holy Spirit is truly God. How important is it for you to envision the Spirit in this way? If so, why is it important? What do you gain with this way of understanding? What do you think people lose if they do not believe that the Spirit is fully God?
4. Some Christians affirm that the Spirit is an agent of God but is not fully God. What would a community gain with this way of thinking? What would a community lose?
5. Whether one believes the Holy Spirit is divine or is a representative of the Divine One, the essential works of the Spirit are much

the same. Which of the following works (as discussed above) are more and which less important to you? Why?
   a. Preserving the chaos
   b. Re-creating
   c. Inspiring leadership
   d. Awakening
   e. Sanctifying
   f. Imparting visions through mystical moments
   g. Making us aware of God's nearness
   h. Working through social process
   i. Baptizing us with the Spirit
   j. Opening us to the feminine dimension of the divine
   k. Continuing to speak, even going beyond the Bible and tradition
6. A challenge to the church is how to identify the work of the Spirit. What criteria could your community use to identify whether experiences result from the Spirit?
7. Which pictures of the Holy Spirit in this chapter do you find most compelling? What makes those pictures compelling? How do those pictures help you?
8. Which images of the Spirit are not compelling to you? Indeed, do you find some of these images unattractive? Why do you not like these images?
9. Voices in the Christian house claim that the Spirit speaks today more authoritatively than the Bible or tradition. Indeed, some claim that the Spirit changes or corrects viewpoints in the Bible. How do you respond to this claim?
10. When do you feel the Holy Spirit most immediately? How do such experiences affect you? Do they help? Empower?

5
The Trinity

The church is filled with language and imagery about the Trinity. Every Sunday some congregations say an affirmation of faith that is structured around the Trinity: "I believe in God . . . I believe in Jesus Christ . . . I believe in the Holy Spirit." The Trinity is represented in various ways—by a triangle, for example, or interlocking circles, a trefoil, a clover leaf—in stained-glass windows, paintings, wood carvings, and the cloths that sometimes drape the Communion table, the pulpit, and the lectern. Yet after hearing laypeople talk about the Trinity in Bible-study groups, I note that many accept the doctrine of the Trinity, but few understand it. As someone said, "I know I'm supposed to believe in this Trinity, but I don't know how to explain it."

Almost from the beginning of the church, members have held different views about the Trinity. One of the most beloved hymns in some parts of the church is "Holy, Holy, Holy." In most hymnals, the first stanza is as follows:

> Holy, holy, holy, Lord God Almighty,
> Early in the morning, our song shall rise to thee.
> Holy, holy, holy, merciful and mighty,
> God in three persons, blessed Trinity.[1]

However, in the hymnal on which I grew up—published by the Christian Church (Disciples of Christ)—the last line was, "God over all,

55

and blessed eternally."[2] Although most members of my denomination are Trinitarian, I have heard that these words were changed to acknowledge the fact that some members do not embrace the Trinity. Indeed, there are whole denominations today that do not subscribe to the doctrine of the Trinity.

THE TRINITY IN THE BIBLE (?)

The word "Trinity" does not appear in the Bible. Virtually all biblical scholars and theologians today agree that the fully developed doctrine of the Trinity is not found in Scripture, though some scholars do think that the Bible contains the seeds of the later doctrine. Other scholars think that the Bible does not contain the notion of the Trinity, and that the church read the doctrine of the Trinity into Scripture. This part of the chapter discusses some of the popular Bible passages that appear most prominently in these discussions.[3]

Genesis 1:26–28: "Let Us Make Humankind in Our Image."

Some Christians take the word "us" to refer to the Trinity when God says, "Let *us* make humankind in our image" (Gen. 1:26, italics ours). However, biblical scholars point out that the "us" in this expression refers to a council of lesser deities or angel-like figures who were with God in heaven. The fact that God was in relationship with others implies that God created human beings for relationship.[4]

Genesis 18:1–19: Three Visitors to Sarah and Abraham

Genesis 18 states that God appeared to Sarah and Abraham at Mamre (Gen. 18:1). The text then indicates that three people arrived at their camp (Gen. 18:2–19). One strain in Christian interpretation identifies the three visitors as the members of the Trinity. However, nothing in the text itself calls for this association. From the perspective of the time, the three visitors are likely God and two angels.

2 Corinthians 13:13: The Grace of Christ, Love of God, and Communion of the Spirit

In 2 Corinthians 13:13, which a minister today sometimes uses as the benediction for a service of worship, Paul blessed the Corinthian congregation with the grace of Christ, the love of God, and the communion of the Spirit. While Paul mentions these three entities, the apostle does not explicitly claim that each of the three is God nor that, together, they are a Trinity. Indeed, Paul elsewhere assumes that God sends Jesus and that the Holy Spirit functions in the ways described in the preceding chapter.

Matthew 28:18–20: Baptizing in the Name of the Father, Son, and Holy Spirit

The language of this passage is more like the later church's language about the Trinity than any other passage in the New Testament. Sometimes known as the Great Commission, this text calls Jesus' followers to make disciples of all nations by "baptizing them in the name of the Father and of the Son and of the Holy Spirit." This passage is the first time this threefold designation appears in early Christian literature.

In the Gospel of Matthew, God is the sovereign actor who works through Jesus to alert the human community to the imminent end of the present age and the coming of the realm of God (e.g., Matt. 4:12–17; 7:21). To be sure, Matthew does speak of Jesus as "'Emmanuel,' which means, 'God is with us'" (Matt. 1:23); but the Gospel writer is here citing Isaiah 7:14, where the name "Immanuel" is to be given to a newborn child whose birth is a sign that God is with the community of Israel in a time of crisis. Similarly, Matthew has a functional view of Jesus as such a sign during the crisis of the end-times. As in the Old Testament, for Matthew the Holy Spirit is the means whereby God works in the world (e.g., Matt. 1:18; 10:20; 12:18).

The congregation to which Matthew wrote considered itself Jewish but was in conflict with some other Jewish communities. Some scholars, then, think that Matthew created the formula "in the name of the Father and the Son and the Holy Spirit" to use at baptism to define the identity of the church. The baptized are related to Judaism (the Father) while carrying on the mission of witnessing to the end-time and the coming of the Realm (the Son) in the power of the Spirit. When Jesus was baptized, God spoke and the Spirit empowered Jesus to witness to the realm (Matt. 3:13–17). Through baptism, the members of the Matthean community are similarly claimed and empowered.

Philippians 2:5–11: Jesus Did Not Count Equality with God a Thing to Be Grasped

Virtually all scholars think that these verses are an ancient Christian hymn that Paul cites, much as a preacher today quotes a hymn from the hymnal in order to help make a point. The apostle encouraged the members of the divided Philippian congregation to recover their sense of having "the same mind" by relating to one another in the same manner as Christ. Instead of acting selfishly or in a conceited manner, they should become servants of one another in the same way that Christ did (Phil. 2:1–11). Christ was preexistent, that is, Christ was with God before the creation of the world and had the opportunity to remain with God in heaven, but, instead, Christ took the form of a servant and came into the world, so that through his death and resurrection God could point the way toward the complete renewal of community.

While Paul was not here primarily commenting on the nature of Christ, the apostle spoke in a way that some Christians have interpreted as meaning that Christ was God by saying, "Though [Christ] was in the form of God, [Christ] did not regard equality with God as something to be exploited" (Phil. 2:6). While this verse has been a minefield of scholarly debate, two things stand out. First, Paul elsewhere clearly understands Christ as an envoy of God, e.g., son of God (Rom. 1:4), wisdom of God (1 Cor. 1:18–25), the one who hands the realm over to God (1 Cor. 15:24), the image of God (2 Cor. 4:4; cf. Gen. 1:26–27). Indeed, Christ will be subjected to God after the apocalypse (1 Cor. 15:28). Second, the Greek term translated "exploited" can also be rendered "grasped." The latter meaning makes more sense here: the preexistent Christ had the opportunity to attempt to grasp or reach for equality with God, but did not.

Colossians 1:15–20: "The Image of the Invisible God"

We can say something similar about Colossians 1:15–20, also a hymn cited by the writer. Colossians was written in the midst of controversy over what the Colossians needed to do in order to enjoy fullness of redeemed life. According to the hymn, through Christ God has reconciled all things (Col. 1:15–20). Therefore, the Colossians are already liberated (1:21–23). They do not need to follow false teachers, whose instruction keeps the congregation in bondage to "the elemental spirits of the universe," powers that distort God's purposes (Col. 2:8–23).

The hymn draws on the wisdom tradition to say that Christ is "the *image* of the invisible God, the firstborn of all creation" (Col. 1:15, italics ours). When the text says that in Christ "all the fullness of God was pleased to dwell" (1:19; cf. 2:9), the meaning is not that Christ became God, but that the power and purposes of God were fully expressed through the death and resurrection of Christ. From the perspective of Colossians, Christ is something like end-time wisdom, through which God brings about reconciliation.

The Gospel of John: The Word Made Flesh

The Fourth Gospel usually speaks of God's sending Jesus, thus indicating that Jesus is God's agent (e.g., John 7:28–29; 8:26, 29). As God sent Jesus, so Jesus sends the disciples (John 13:20). God is greater than Jesus (John 14:28). Jesus ascends to God, whom Jesus describes as "my Father and your Father" (John 20:17). Jesus and God are one (John 10:30); God dwells in Jesus, and Jesus in God (10:38; cf. 17:22–24), yet the oneness in view is oneness of purpose, as in "My spouse and I are one with respect to a particular issue."

Most scholars say that two passages declare that Jesus is God. In my view, however, neither text calls for that conclusion. John 1:1 says, "The Word was with God, and the Word was God." The Greek has the article ("the") with "the Word" but not with "God." In Greek, the presence of the article denotes specificity (*the* Word), whereas the absence of the article can indicate nature or force. Moreover, interpreting a biblical passage the Jewish writer Philo, who lived just before the writing of the Fourth Gospel, notes that the text indicates "Him Who is truly God by means of the article saying, 'Who appeared to thee in the place' not 'of the God' but simply 'of God.' Here it [the text] gives the title of 'God' to His Chief Word."[5] John 1:1, then, could be translated, "The Word was of divine origin and force," meaning that it came from God and operated under God's authority. A similar approach applies to the words of Thomas in response to seeing the resurrected Jesus: "My Lord and my God!" (John 20:28). Beyond that, John envisions the Spirit not as equal with God and Jesus, but as their servant.

THE TRINITY IN THE HISTORY OF THE CHURCH

Although the Trinity is taken for granted in many corners today, the doctrine of the Trinity as we know it was not explicitly formulated until the fourth and fifth centuries. The Council of Nicaea (325 CE) asserts the doctrine of the Trinity but is vague on the relationship of the Holy Spirit to the Trinity. The Council of Chalcedon (451 CE) was much more explicit regarding the relationship of the Spirit to God and Jesus. While these councils settled the issues around the Trinity for many believers, differences regarding how to interpret the Trinity continued. One of the most important points in this discussion is that all participants regarded themselves as monotheists. The doctrine of the Trinity is intended to show that God is *one*.[6]

God Adopted Jesus the Human Being (Adoptionism)

Many Christians in the second and third centuries of the Common Era believed that before the creation of the world God was a singular entity and that Christ did not then exist with God. Jesus was born as only a human being, though many adoptionists say that Christ lived an exemplary life. At a specific point, God adopted the human being Jesus for God's special purposes. For example, some adoptionists believed that the apostle Paul taught that God adopted Jesus at the resurrection, while others said that the Gospel of Mark taught that God adopted Jesus at the baptism. Some adoptionists thought that God adopted Jesus as a special agent, much like a prophet. At the moment of adoption the human Jesus began a special work for God. Many adoptionists taught, further, that at adoption Christ became divine.

Jesus Was Divine but Was Created before the World (Arianism)

Christians today sometimes use the word Arianism to refer generally to any perception that Christ is not fully God in the Trinitarian sense. However, Arianism has a more technical meaning. Arius (ca. 250–336 CE) was an Egyptian thinker who went beyond the idea that God adopted Christ after the incarnation, but stopped short of teaching that God and Christ are both eternal beings. Arius taught that God always existed and that God begot Christ before the creation of the world. God and Christ are not the same being and do not share the same substance (as in classical Trinitarian thought). After being begotten, Christ was divine but served God and worked jointly with God to create the Holy Spirit. For its part, the Spirit served Christ in the same way that Christ served God. Christ is a lesser entity than God, with the Holy Spirit a little lesser entity than Jesus.

God Appearing in Different Modes, One at a Time (Modalism)

Modalists believe that God is one, but that God manifests Godself successively in one of three different modes—God, Christ, and the Holy Spirit. God is never, at the same time, manifest as Father, Christ, and Spirit. To use a crude analogy, God would be manifest as the Father, and then turn off the Father and turn on manifestation as Christ. God would then turn off Christ and turn on the Holy Spirit. The modes are manifest one at a time. This interpretation is sometimes called Sabellianism (after Sabellius, whose high-water mark was about 217–220 CE and who was a chief proponent of this view). The Father is not higher than Christ or the Spirit. Each mode is equal in power with the others, but only one mode can be manifest at a given time.

An aspect of modalism associated with Sabellius disturbed many Christians of his day, namely, the idea that God suffered on the cross in the mode of Christ. Christians who objected to the idea of God suffering held views of God influenced by Greek philosophy (such as the notion of God as unmoved mover, discussed in chapter 2). The idea that God suffers is called Patripassianism.[7] In an interesting reversal, many Christians today (without becoming modalists) insist that God incarnate in Jesus suffered on the cross, for such suffering shows that God fully understands what it means to be human. We can pray in greater solidarity to a God who has experienced our situation than to an unmoved mover.

God and Christ Are One God (Binitarianism)

The name Binitarianism implies two persons within the one Godhead. The Father and Christ are both God. They existed eternally, and neither created the other. Binitarianism views the Holy Spirit much like the Old Testament: the Spirit is the representative of the Godhead who brings the will of the Godhead to pass. However, the Spirit is not God. Some forms of Binitarianism are loosely called Semi-Arianism because they go beyond Arius in claiming that the Father and Christ are fully one God, but they stop short of Trinitarianism by denying that the Holy Spirit is part of the Godhead. Macedonianism (a fourth-century movement whose name comes from Bishop Macedonius) was such a group, whose adherents were even known as "spirit fighters," that is, those who fought the idea that the Holy Spirit is part of the Godhead.

The Church in the West: God Is One in Substance While Three Persons

As noted already, the doctrine of the Trinity, not fully articulated until the Council of Chalcedon (451), brought some later additions. The fundamental intention of this doctrine is to assert that God is one. Yet, the doctrine of the Trinity is hard to describe because our language has difficulty precisely capturing what is meant in the notion of God as one substance while being three persons (Father, Son, and Holy Spirit). We sometimes say that God is one-in-three and three-in-one. The English word "person" is a little misleading, however, because common usage today implies a much greater level of distinction than is present in the Trinity. Whenever we speak of the three, we imply the one Godhead. Whenever we speak of one person, we presuppose all three.

The notion of person in Trinitarianism is similar to that of role, sometimes expressed in shorthand as creator (Father), redeemer (Christ), and sustainer (Spirit). In Modalism the individual persons of God are manifest one after another. In Trinitarianism, the fullness of the Father is present at all times in the Son and in the Spirit. For example, in his role as Christ the Redeemer, God the Father, God the Son, and God the Holy Spirit were fully present.

The Nicene Affirmation also says that the Spirit "proceeds from the Father and the Son." The phrase "and the Son" was not part of the original Affirmation but was added many years later to assert (against Arius) that Jesus is of the same substance as the Father. The Affirmation, of course, presumed that the Spirit is also of the same substance.

The Church in the East: The Spirit Proceeds Only from the Father

Some churches in the eastern part of the Mediterranean did not accept the additional phrase "and the Son" with respect to the affirmation that the Holy Spirit proceeds "from the Father and the Son." These churches objected (1) that the additional phrase was not found in the Bible, (2) that the addition was made by a small group without the whole church's being able to discuss it, and (3) that it suggested division within the Godhead. By omitting the phrase "and [from] the Son," the church could affirm the absolute singularity of God as the source of both the Son and the Spirit.[8]

Although differences over the phrase "and the Son" may seem minuscule to many people today, they were huge in antiquity. Prior to 1054, the church in the Mediterranean basin and Europe was one church, but in that year, the church split into eastern and western parts, with the eastern churches becoming the Orthodox communions and the western parts becoming the Roman Catholic Church and, later, the Protestant churches. Disagreement over the addition of the phrase "and the Son" was one of the reasons for the split.

THE TRINITY IN THE CONTEMPORARY CHURCH

While the majority of Christian denominations and movements today officially accept the Nicaean-Constantinopolitan belief that God is one substance in three persons, we find diversity of attitudes toward the doctrine of the Trinity among and within churches and among individual Christians. Most contemporary viewpoints are similar to those in the history of the church. Not surprisingly, many Trinitarian churches say that the Trinity is a mystery, not in the sense that it is a puzzle, but in the sense that its truth is so deep that we cannot fully explain or express it.

God Is One Substance in Three Persons: Essential and Economic Trinity

Much current discussion of the Trinity focuses on the distinction between interpreting the Trinity in essential and in economic terms. Of course, these are the same Trinity, but the two perspectives are simply two ways of highlighting different aspects of the same thing, as if one looks at a statute in an art gallery from the left and then from the right. The essential Trinity implies the economic perspective, and the economic Trinity implies the nature of the essential Trinity.

The essential Trinity calls attention to the essence of God in Godself.[9] When focusing on the essential Trinity, Christians seek to explore the internal life of God. Of course, we cannot look into the Godhead with a microscope to examine the actual essence of the Trinity, so Christians rely on the Bible, on the testimony of church leaders, and on the experience of the economic Trinity to try to understand as much of the essence of God as possible. The scholarly consensus in this discussion today is that the three persons in the Trinity exist in a relationship of complete love, equality, and mutuality.

The root of the ancient Greek word "economic" is "household." This way of speaking about the Trinity makes an analogy between the life of the Trinity and the many operations that were necessary for a household to function in antiquity. The economic Trinity focuses on what God does in the world. When moving from the essential to the economic Trinity, the shift in perspective is from who God is in Godself to what we experience of God's actions in the world. Because of the limitations of human finitude and sin, we can never know completely the essence of God, though God's actions in the world reveal the core of the divine character.

God Is One Substance in Three Persons: Model for Human Community

The historical context of a Christian community often helps a community become sensitive to particular aspects of Christian doctrine. One of the aching issues of contemporary life is fractured human community among nations, racial/ethnic groups, the genders, and even within the self. Drawing from the Trinity in both essential and economic terms, many Christians today view the Trinity as the model for human community (and for the relationship of humankind and nature).

The essence of God as Trinity is three persons in the Godhead in completely loving, egalitarian, mutually supportive relationship. God in the economic Trinity acts in the world in these ways. Human beings are made in the image of God. Consequently, human beings are, at the core of our essence, made for loving, egalitarian, mutually supportive community. Human relationships with one another, therefore, should embody the relationships within the Godhead.

As a side note, when I first encountered the term economic Trinity I thought it was unfortunate, because in contemporary North America the word "economic" usually refers to money and material life. However, occasional Trinitarian thinkers today play on both associations to contend that the economy of God is the model for how people and material resources (including money) should work together throughout life in the world. From this latter point of view, the term "economic" calls attention to an important aspect of the work of the Trinity.

One God: One Person (Unitarians)

Some people contend that the doctrine of the Trinity is logically incoherent. What sense does it make to claim that God is simultaneously one substance and three persons? Moreover, these thinkers contend that the doctrine of the Trinity is unnecessary. We can account for creation, redemption, the sustaining of the world, God's empathy with humankind, and God's will for human communities to live in love without the doctrine of the Trinity. Such folk are unitarian, that is, they emphasize the unity or oneness of God, but do not accept the Trinity.

Many unitarians belong to the Unitarian Universalist Association. Many congregations are called "Christian Unitarians," with many holding beliefs similar to those of the churches of the period of the New Testament. They regard Jesus as prophet, teacher, and even redeemer. They regard the Holy Spirit as God's living agent. The hymns, Bible readings, and sermons are often similar to those found in conventional Christian congregations, while emphasizing unitarian and universalist themes. In addition, some Christians in other denominations hold similar perspectives. For example, I know a few members of my own

denomination, the Christian Church (Disciples of Christ), who subscribe to such views.

Other Unitarian-Universalist congregations maintain a greater sense
of distance from the Christian tradition and from Jesus. Indeed, they
manifest great diversity in beliefs that can lean more to philosophy or
Buddhism than to the Jewish-Christian tradition.

Jesus Is God (Oneness Pentecostalism)

Oneness Pentecostalism affirms the oneness of God. However, it does
not accept the doctrine of the Trinity nor is it unitarian in the sense
just discussed.[10] For this group, Jesus as presented in the New Testament is God. The God of the Old Testament is Jesus known by other
names. Thus, Jesus created the world, called Sarai and Abram, liberated
the children of Israel from bondage, and so on. The Holy Spirit is now
Jesus present and acting in the One. As the name implies, the Oneness Pentecostal churches typically worship in an expressive Pentecostal
way, with emphasis on speaking in tongues.

God and Jesus Are One God (Binitarianism)

Binitarianism is a living option on the spectrum of Christian belief. The
following churches are binitarian: the Church of God (Seventh Day), the
United Church of God, and the Living Church of God. These churches
are stoutly not bitheistic, emphasizing that both the Father and the Son
are God. The Holy Spirit is the representative of the Godhead carrying
out the will of the Father and the Son. Many binitarians believe that the
New Testament presents God and Jesus in binitarian relationship.

Two Gods: One in Purpose (Bitheism)

The bitheist viewpoint, held by the Jehovah's Witnesses, is that God
and Jesus are each a separate God, hence they are two Gods and not
two-in-one (or one-in-two). Jesus is a lesser God than the Father. Nevertheless, the two Gods share the same purpose and are completely
coordinated. For bitheists, the Holy Spirit is not part of the Godhead,
but is an agent who serves both the Father and the Son.

Three Gods: One in Purpose (Tritheism)

The Church of Jesus Christ of Latter Day Saints (Mormons) is the only church, to my knowledge, to be tritheistic. This church believes that God, Jesus, and the Holy Spirit are three distinct deities who are, nevertheless, one in purpose, and who relate with one another in unique ways. The three gods are distinct individuals but perfect in unity. Many Christians view both bitheism and tritheism as heresies.

QUESTIONS FOR DISCUSSION

1. Recalling the notion of embedded faith in chapter 1, what is your embedded understanding of the Trinity?
2. What fresh thoughts or questions about the Trinity has this chapter stirred?
3. If you are a Trinitarian, what do you find most compelling about the idea of the Trinity? Which understandings of the Trinity do you find most persuasive? How might the notion of the Trinity help you? What questions do you have about the Trinity? What do you find not so compelling about it?
4. If you are not a Trinitarian, to what other viewpoints in this chapter are you most attracted: Unitarian? Modalist? Binitarian? Arian? In comparison to Trinitarianism, what do you think you gain with your belief? What do you lose?
5. This chapter concentrated on the Nicene Affirmation of Faith. Over the years, churches have generated many more affirmations. Does your church subscribe to the Nicene Affirmation? Does your church have additional affirmations of faith? If so, it would be good to read the different affirmations alongside one another and to compare and contrast them. What do you notice? Does the affirmation of your church really describe your understanding of the Trinity?
6. Some Christians contend that affirmations of faith (such as the Nicene) articulate with precision what Christians must believe. Others think that such affirmations are more poetic and evocative, suggesting general attitudes about God and life rather than prescribing specific beliefs. Where do you fall on this spectrum?

6

God's Ultimate Purposes

When I was serving as a minister in a local congregation, I once reviewed program resources for helping churches organize for evangelism. One program I examined taught members of an evangelism committee who would call in the homes of nonchurch people to ask the following question: "If you died tonight, are you sure you would wake up in heaven?" If the person being questioned did not answer "Yes," the book contained suggestions on what callers could say that might lead to a firm "Yes." The writers of this program believed that God's ultimate purpose is for individual human beings to join God in heaven, where they will be reunited with family members and friends for eternity. This program assumed that some who die will not be in heaven, but will awaken to eternal punishment.

My impression is that many people in congregations share this belief, that God's ultimate purpose is to save individuals from perdition and to welcome them into heaven.[1] But this belief is only one of several interpretations of God's ultimate purposes. While nearly all these perspectives involve individuals, some also include communities and even the natural world.

In the following, I take account of God's ultimate purposes for both the individual and the larger social and natural worlds. Often these dimensions (individual and world) are related, so separating them is only for the sake of simplifying discussion.

GOD'S ULTIMATE PURPOSES IN THE BIBLE

Christians sometimes think the Bible is a continuous story with two chapters. Chapter 1: Human beings long for eternal life (Old Testament). Chapter 2: God fulfills this longing by providing eternal life through Christ (New Testament). In fact, however, the Bible contains several views of God's ultimate purposes.

God Aims for People to Have a Blessed Life in the Present

Most of the Old Testament presumes that God's ultimate purpose is for the human family to enjoy fullness of life in the present. By and large the writers of the Old Testament did not envision special blessedness or punishment beyond the present world.

The blessed life was one in which people lived according to the covenant that God made with Israel. At the personal level, the good life consisted of family, abundant food, clothing, shelter, and other resources necessary for a secure life. Moreover, God sought to bless Israel as a *community* and to bless other communities. Micah captures the intertwining of the personal and the communal. "[God] shall judge between many peoples, and shall arbitrate between strong nations far away; they shall beat their swords into plowshares, and their spears into pruning hooks; nation shall not lift up sword against nation, neither shall they learn war any more; but they shall all sit under their own fig trees, and no one shall make them afraid" (Mic. 4:3–4).

Although the Old Testament contains different forms of the covenant, they all acknowledge that God graciously chose Israel and provided instructions for Israel to live a blessed life.[2] Community members were to provide for widows, orphans, and persons visiting from other communities. When things interrupted this life—such as invasion by other nations or the community's own idolatry and practice of injustice—God sought to regenerate Israel. Even when God condemned Israel, the purpose of the judgment was usually to awaken repentance. God's ultimate purpose was to restore the people.

Sheol: A Shadowy World of the Dead

While most writers of the Old Testament believed that God's ultimate aim is to bless people in the present, most of the same writers also thought that the spirits of the dead went to Sheol, a place that was neither heaven (reward) nor hell (punishment), but a shadowy space in which all people had the same quality of existence.[3] The Old Testament sometimes speaks of the dead going "down" to Sheol as if it were located beneath the earth or the sea. Inhabitants of Sheol experienced little pleasure or pain. Existence in Sheol was dark and silent, even grim, and continued forever.

The Future (and Present) Realm of God

The only certain reference in the Old Testament to God's purposes extending beyond the present world is Daniel 12:1–3 (ca. 165 BCE).[4] "Many of those who sleep in the dust of the earth shall awake, some to everlasting life, and some to shame and everlasting contempt. Those who are wise shall shine like the brightness of the sky, and those who lead many to righteousness, [shall shine] like the stars forever and ever."

This passage is part of the movement we discussed in connection with Jesus as end-time prophet (above). These writings presume that the present world is broken beyond repair. God will destroy this world and create a new one called the realm of God where all things will occur according to God's purposes: love, peace, justice, abundance, mutual support, and harmony between humankind and nature.

For many of these writers, at death the individual loses consciousness, but (per Daniel) when the new world comes, all individuals are raised to a great judgment when God welcomes the faithful into God's realm but consigns the unfaithful to punishment in hell. The self is not divided into parts (such as soul and body), but is a whole. In the old age, the self decays, but when raised, the self has a new kind of body that does not wear out.

The idea that God's ultimate purpose is to end the present world and inaugurate a new one is the backdrop for Paul, Mark, Matthew, Luke-Acts, and most of the rest of the New Testament.[5] According to the early Christians, the ministry, death, and resurrection of Jesus Christ signal the fact that the end of the present and the beginning of the new is about to occur. Indeed, the earliest followers of Jesus believed that his ministry anticipated aspects of the realm in the healings, fellowship meals, and Jesus' resurrection. Scholars sometimes refer to this phenomenon as the present and future, the already and not yet. In the realm the faithful receive resurrection bodies and never die.

The Self Follows the Way to God's Heaven

As noted earlier, many Greek thinkers believed that life had two spheres, which can be figuratively represented as a two-story universe with heaven above and the world below. Heaven was eternal, while the world was a flimsy copy of heaven. The human being was composed of two parts—soul and body. A major goal of life was for the nonmaterial soul to migrate from the body at death to join the heavenly world. Many Christians today believe similarly.

A modified form of this thought is behind the Gospel and Letters of John. For John, heaven is a domain of God, life, love, truth, unity, and similar qualities. The world is a domain of the devil, hate, darkness, falsehood, and fractiousness. God's ultimate purpose is for the essence of the self to leave the present world and to journey to heaven. For example, in John 14:2–3 when the Johannine Jesus says, "In my Father's house there are many dwelling places. If it were not so, would I have told you that I go to prepare a place for you? And if I go and prepare a place for you, I will come again and take you to myself, so that where I am, you may be also." Jesus ascends to heaven ("my Father's house") to prepare spaces for his followers who will leave the world and ascend to heaven.

Until the soul ascends to heaven, God infuses Jesus' followers who are still in the world with the qualities of heaven. Jesus says, "I came that they may have life, and have it abundantly" (John 10:10). However, "those who do not believe [in Jesus] are condemned already" (John 3:18).[6]

Limited and Universal Salvation

Christians today sometimes use the terms limited salvation and universal salvation in connection with God's ultimate purposes. While these terms are not found in the Bible, they have a utility in setting out different perspectives.[7] The term limited salvation refers to the possibility that only a limited number of people will be with God in the new realm or in heaven. Some people are not welcomed into the realm but are sent to punishment. Some people do not make the journey into heaven but are condemned or are otherwise denied full participation in God's ultimate purposes. Most of the biblical writers believed in limited salvation.

By contrast, universal salvation refers to every human being's receiving the benefit of God's ultimate purposes.[8] Universal salvation holds not simply that God offers salvation to everyone but that God actually brings every person into heaven, into the coming realm or otherwise bestows ultimate blessing. Occasional biblical documents, such as Ephesians, can be interpreted as advocating universal salvation.

GOD'S ULTIMATE PURPOSES
IN THE HISTORY OF THE CHURCH

The church in history adapted pictures of God's ultimate purposes found in the Bible. But congregations have been more interested in the destiny of the individual than that of the world. Between the time of the Bible and today, many Christians have combined the two main viewpoints from the New Testament. Reflecting Greek influence, they believed that at death the soul is separated from the body and goes to be with God in heaven. Reflecting the realm of God as a new world, they believed that God would carry out the final judgment, at which time the soul would be reunited with the body. Past Christians did not believe in these ideas simply as "pie in the sky by-and-by," but as the means whereby God's love and justice would be finally and fully expressed.

Union with God: The Orthodox Perspective

The Orthodox churches in the past and present combine aspects of the journey of the soul to heaven with the coming of a new world. At the time of death, the soul experiences a partial judgment, that is, God gives the soul a partial experience of what lies ahead for eternity. When Christ returns, the final judgment will take place. With respect

to God's ultimate purposes for the individual, the Orthodox communions believe in a process called *theosis,* or deification, through which
a Christian can participate in the divine life increasingly in the present
and more intensely after death. Christians do not become God, but
they do participate in the divine energies. Heaven is the state of endless
experience of God's fathomless love. The Orthodox continue to pray
for the dead, though the Orthodox churches do not specify what or
how the prayers of the living affect the ongoing existence of the dead.
The Orthodox trust that God will do what is right with the dead.

The Orthodox churches anticipate that God will ultimately trans-
figure the cosmos so that, like the deified human being, it will fully
express the divine purposes. The Orthodox churches do not speculate
regarding how or when this event will take place.

God does not directly punish those who reject God, but casts them
into the infinity of love. In the midst of God's love, the rejection of
God is its own punishment. The awareness of denying God is thus the
equivalent of the hell of fire and brimstone.

Purgatory: A Roman Catholic Touch

The Roman Catholic Church subscribes to a version both of the journey of the soul to heaven and the notion of a final judgment. At death,
the soul of the faithful leaves the body. Roman Catholics believe that
God then makes a particular judgment about each particular individual
and assigns each soul to one of three places: (1) heaven, (2) purgatory,
or (3) hell. Only a few souls go directly to heaven, because they can
do so only if they die with the debt created by sin completely paid.
Consequently, most souls must spend some time in purgatory. After
purgation, the faithful soul enters heaven and dwells with God until
the final judgment. The soul sent to hell after purgatory suffers until
the final judgment. At that judgment, God will reunite the souls and
bodies of those in heaven and in hell. Those from heaven will live forever with God as the complete selves (bodies joined to souls), while the
unfaithful are condemned as whole selves to the punishment of hell.
Souls welcomed into heaven experience the beatific vision, that is, the
vision of God's own being. The soul in heaven has but one desire: the
pure longing to be with God.

Between death and entry into heaven, then, the soul makes a stop
in purgatory. At death, those who will join God in heaven but die

while still weighed down by sin go to purgatory, an intermediate place between life on earth and life in heaven. Purgatory is not a place of eternal punishment but, as the name implies, is an arena in which souls are purified for life with God. The prayers of the faithful can strengthen the individual in purgatory.

Traditional Roman Catholic teaching described hell as a place of punishment, and often depicted it as an arena of fire and brimstone. Some voices in Catholic theology, especially in recent generations, speak of hell more as a state of estrangement from God than as a place of punishment. Indeed, some of the latter see going to hell less as God's directive and more as human beings' excluding themselves from God's love.

The final judgment occurs at a time of God's own choosing. At that time, the soul is reunited with the body so that the whole self can experience eternally either the beatific vision (heaven) or punishment. The Catholic Church teaches that, in connection with the final judgment, God's ultimate purposes include transforming the earth (the physical universe) into a new earth. The new world will be similar to Eden.

Most Protestants: The Soul Goes to Heaven Awaiting the Final Judgment

Most Protestants, at least at the popular level, have shared the general combination of the two basic understandings of God's purposes set forth in the New Testament: The self is a combination of soul and body; at death, the soul goes either to heaven or to hell. For Protestants, heaven is the place where God dwells, so that the faithful are forever fully in the presence of God. Hell, by contrast, is a place of punishment which Protestants often envision as a literal place of fire. Protestant churches do not follow the most distinctive teachings of the Orthodox (*theosis*) or the Roman Catholics (purgatory). Indeed, most Protestants reject the idea of an intermediate state (such as purgatory) between the moment of death and full entry into the next life. While living Protestants may give thanks for the dead and pray for their own relationships with the dead (for example, praying for forgiveness for a wrong done to the dead), Protestants do not tend to pray *for* the ultimate disposition of the dead, nor do Protestants pray to the dead for help in the present. In addition, most Protestants in history believed that Jesus will return and that God will carry out a final judgment. Many Protestants continue to believe this way.

Universal Salvation

Across the history of the church, most Christians have advocated limited salvation (as above). Most churches have insisted that people must believe in Jesus Christ in order to be saved. But occasional Christians have believed in universal salvation. For example, Julian of Norwich (1342–1416) believed that God loved and would save all: "I [God] will make all things well, I shall make all things well, I may make all things well and I can make all things well; and you will see that yourself, that all things will be well."[9] Universalism was especially potent in Germany and England in the sixteenth and seventeenth centuries, with active voices making their way to North America. Indeed, the Universalist Church in the United States (which traces its roots to the 1740s) has often seen a correlation between its belief that God loves all and ethical witness. Its members opposed slavery because they believed that God intended fullness of blessing at all stages in life.

Death as the End of Human Consciousness

In the history of the church, only a handful of people (relatively speaking) believed that death is simply the end of human consciousness. Their viewpoint is similar in structure to that of the majority of writers of the Old Testament: God's ultimate purposes must be fulfilled in the present life or (as far as the individual is concerned), not at all. Adherents of this way of thinking were most numerous at the dawn of the Enlightenment.

GOD'S ULTIMATE PURPOSES
IN THE CONTEMPORARY CHURCH

Most of the options we have seen in history are also present in the church today, especially the views of the Orthodox and Roman Catholic churches and many Protestant churches. In addition, the 1800s and 1900s brought forth a plethora of different forms and timetables of God's ultimate purposes, especially related to the second coming, that are prominent today. Several of these categories overlap.

Generic Belief: Some Individuals Go to Heaven and Others to Hell

I find that many Christians have a generic belief that God's ultimate purpose is to save the individual soul. At death, the soul leaves the body and goes to heaven or hell. In heaven, the soul is reunited with family and friends, while hell is either a place of active punishment or a condition of estrangement.[10] Many people also have a vague sense that Jesus will return. People often hold such beliefs without thinking carefully about them. But at the time of death, grieving people often seek comfort through them.

Figurative Language and Limited Language: Heaven and Hell, the Second Coming

I also find that a good many Christians use the language of heaven, hell, and Jesus' second coming not to refer to specific places to which one goes after death, but figuratively to speak of experiences in the present that may (or may not) extend beyond death or in a new world. For example, people sometimes speak of "heaven on earth." Some people take the language of Jesus' coming again to refer to the ways that Jesus comes now through friends, groups, social movements, and events in nature. Indeed, someone recently professed to me not to be concerned about the details of an afterlife or a new world. This person observed that we do not have firm evidence regarding what happens after death, but that our awareness of God's love and trustworthiness in this life and world is basis enough for trusting God with what happens at death and beyond.

The Millennialisms: Pre/Post/Amillennialism

Some Christians, especially in evangelical circles, use the language of millenarianism for God's ultimate purposes. This discussion concerns when Christ will return from heaven and reign on earth for a thousand years—an event mentioned in Revelation 20:4–6—and the relationship of that millennial reign to the final coming of Christ. I discuss the main forms of millenarianism under one heading for comparison and contrast. Some of these notions are similar to others discussed below.

Premillennialism. A very popular mode of thinking today, premillennialism did not appear until John Nelson Darby (1800–1882) divided history into dispensations (large eras of time).[11] The last dispensation is the millennium. This movement is called premillennialism because its adherents believe that Christ will return before the literal thousand-year millennium. After the millennium, Christ will return a last time for the final judgment.[12] Biblical scholars in the tradition in which I move agree that no single author in Scripture puts forward the comprehensive premillennial time line. The "Left Behind" series of books and movies is the most popular exposition of this viewpoint today.

Postmillennialism. Advocates of postmillennialism believe that Christ will return after the realm has been established on the earth. God is at work in the present through human beings and social movements to make the present world into the realm of God. Postmillennialists (many of whom do not think the millennium is literally a thousand-year reign) envision the millennium as a time of social transformation, with the world becoming a golden age.

Amillennialism. A key aspect of amillennialism is tied to the use of "a" in the sense of negation: not a literal thousand-year reign. Amillennialists believe the millennium in Revelation 20 is symbolic of the rule of Christ. For amillennialism, Christ is already reigning. Some amillennialists think that we are living under the rule of Christ now (the millennium) but that Christ will physically return a final time. Other amillennialists believe that Christ will not literally return again. For some, the church is God's realm, while for others this realm is present in the heart of the believer and in groups and movements that conform to God's purposes.

Preterism should be included in this discussion. The name Preterist comes from a Latin word for past, so it is not surprising that its followers believe that the final events in salvation took place in the past. The most important of these are the birth, ministry, death, and resurrection of Christ, the destruction of the Temple, and the fall of Rome. These key events (and others) were predicted in Scripture as the key events of the last days, and they have already taken place. Consequently, the realm of God is already here and the faithful live under that aegis. Preterists do not believe that Jesus will come again in the future, because they believe that the events associated with the second coming have already occurred.

God's Realm: Present (and Future)

Some Christians subscribe to versions of the idea of God's ultimate purpose being to re-create the world as a realm of love, peace, justice, mutuality, dignity, freedom, and abundance. The realm of God becomes momentarily manifest in the present in specific moments where its social values are embodied. Some people believe that, in the future, Christ will physically return and complete the redemption of the world; others are not sure whether Christ will return "on the clouds," but they do believe God will somehow bring about the realm in fullness. Others believe that God is always present to lure the world toward the realm.

Liberation: Racial/Ethnic, Gender-linked, Political, Economic

A contemporary school of thought called liberation theology shares perspectives with God's realm: present (and future), but deserves its own discussion because it concentrates especially on God's ultimate purpose, liberating individuals and communities from social and systemic forces that oppress people. Among the most widespread distortions of God's purposes are racism, sexism, ageism, economic exploitation, political injustice and repression, nationalism, neocolonialism, heterosexism, and environmental destruction. Some liberation theologians think that social liberation now is a limited manifestation of the realm, and that ultimate and permanent liberation will come only with a world-transforming event such as the second coming of Jesus. These believers regard death as the most powerful form of repression, so that we can be fully liberated only when we are free from death. Other liberationists think that social liberation in the present is the ultimate expression of God's purposes.

At Death the Self Dies and Awaits
the Resurrection and the New Realm

Some churches believe that at death the self loses consciousness and awaits the general resurrection, at which time God will also regenerate the world. The Seventh Day Adventists, for instance, believe that consciousness is not possible apart from the body. At death, the lights go out and God turns them on again only when Jesus returns and raises the body.

Consciousness Alive Forever in God

A small group of Christians does not accept either the idea of history being divided into two ages or the idea of heaven and hell as locations above and below. They see existence as an ongoing process in which all things take place in God. At death, the self goes out of existence. However, since God lives forever, and since all things take place in God and God remembers all things, human consciousness is alive forever in God.

Within God, a certain kind of judgment takes place. All memories of everything that all human beings have done and felt are always conscious in God. When individuals die, their consciousness thus becomes present to the consciousness of all that they have done. In the pure atmosphere of God's love, that consciousness confronts the ways in which we defied the divine purposes and we are aware of what we have done. We experience that moment as one of judgment. Yet, it is only one moment in the larger interior life of God in which God's pure, unbounded love draws the individual consciousness, now purged, into harmony with all others. In God, each individual occasion is ultimately brought into harmony with God's deepest purposes, for all things to relate together in love and mutual support. In this way of thinking, all human beings must thus take personal responsibility for their bad choices in life, but their future prospects in God are not defined by those choices.

Limited and Universal Salvation

The contemporary church contains viewpoints on limited and universal salvation as explained previously. My impression is that the percentage of Christians who believe in universal salvation is small but growing. However, in the contemporary era, people do not always define what they mean by "salvation." If one is to speak meaningfully of universal salvation, then the notion itself needs to be spelled out.

Death Is the End of Human Consciousness

Some people believe that death is the end of human consciousness. For them, God's purposes must be fulfilled in the present. Of course, understandings of God's ultimate purposes vary from personal fulfillment to social transformation.

QUESTIONS FOR DISCUSSION

1. Recalling the notion of embedded faith in chapter 1, what is your embedded understanding of God's ultimate purposes, especially regarding heaven (and hell) and the possibility of God's destroying this world and beginning a new one?

2. Has this chapter prompted fresh thoughts or questions about God's ultimate purposes?

3. Interpretations of God's ultimate purposes can be clustered in five main groups. What do you see as the most inviting qualities of each of the possibilities below? What are your questions about each one? Can you choose one that is closest to your current thinking? Explain why.

    a. Present purposes: God's ultimate purposes take place in this life (with nothing beyond).

    b. Future purpose: God will end the present age and replace it with the social and cosmic realm of God.

    c. Present and future: The signs of the realm are manifest in the present, but the new world will come in the future.

    d. Heaven and hell: At death God takes faithful souls to heaven and consigns the unfaithful to hell.

    e. The consciousness of the self is alive forever in God.

4. What do you see as the relationship between God's activity and human activity in fulfilling God's ultimate purposes? What does God do and what do we do?

5. If you believe that something lies beyond death or beyond the present social world, do you think God's ultimate purposes will be limited to a few people, or will they be universal, that is, for all? Why?

6. What changes in your individual life do you need to make in order to participate with (or to be ready for) your interpretation of God's ultimate purposes?

7

The Church

How we spend our money often indicates our priorities. The committee responsible for preparing the church budget is meeting. Funds are limited, and several proposals for new initiatives are on the table. A member of a mission team has returned from Haiti after floods have ravaged the country, and says, "We must send every available dollar to Haiti." The property committee points out that the congregation has delayed replacing the church roof for several years, while another group wants to renovate the church parlor. Someone wonders whether the congregation should build its own school so the children in the congregation will not be exposed to worldly influence as they are in the public schools. When someone puts forward the possibility of the congregation's cooperating with the synagogue down the street, someone else suggests that they include the nearby mosque. "And what about the Bahais?" Still another idea is floated under the banner of "We don't do enough to convert people. We should create a coordinated public relations program (internet, radio, television, billboards, newspapers, and the local community magazine) to invite people to join the church."

How will the committee decide which proposals to accept? Likely the members will evaluate the proposals on the basis of what they understand as the nature and purpose of the church—that is, what the church is (nature) and what it is called to do (purpose).[1]

UNDERSTANDINGS OF THE CHURCH IN THE BIBLE

The earliest Christian communities did not think of themselves as a new religion but rather believed that they were extending the ministry of Israel. Consequently, we must first understand the nature and purpose of Israel before turning to how the earliest followers of Jesus perceived themselves.

Israel Chosen to Represent God among the Gentiles

One group in Israel frames the entire story of Israel this way: God chose Israel so that Israel can show the way to blessing to the other peoples of the world. Israel did not incorporate itself (so to speak), but was constituted by God, who chose Israel not for special status, but to carry out a particular mission. In Genesis 12:1–3, God calls Sarai and Abram to become a special human family with the promise that God will bless them and make them a great nation. The Priestly thinkers summarize the purpose of this call succinctly: "In you [Israel] all the families of the earth shall be blessed." This perspective is stated similarly in Exodus 19:5–6. At Sinai, the Priestly God says, "Now therefore, if you obey my voice and keep my covenant, you shall be my treasured possession out of all the peoples. Indeed, the whole earth is mine, but you shall be for me a priestly [dominion] and a holy nation." The life of the people as a whole is to perform a priestly function in behalf of the other nations of the world. Isaiah entwines these themes in a memorable image. "I am [God], I have called you in righteousness . . . ; I have given you as a covenant to the people, a light to the nations" (Isa. 42:6). Israel is to model the life that God wishes for all. The nations (the Gentiles) should be able to look at Israel and discern the way to blessing.

These writers regarded God as sovereign and at work among all peoples. They sought, then, to help Israel name and respond appropriately to God's work on the larger world stage. Isaiah, for example, points to Cyrus, the ruler of Persia, as God's tool to free Israel from exile (Isa. 44:21–28; 45:1–17).

Israel to Maintain Its Own Identity in the Face of Threat

Another group also emphasized God's love for Israel. Writing at a time when the community was threatened by invasion and the prospect of exile, they emphasized that, in order to survive as a people, Israel needed to obey the Law (Torah). Israel's mission was to follow the Law faithfully and to avoid compromising with the other nations, especially in regard to idolatry and injustice. Though these thinkers do not directly state that Israel has a responsibility to the other peoples, the mutual faithfulness of God and Israel should testify to other nations that the God of Israel is more powerful than any other deity (e.g., Deut. 4:5–8; 29:22–28).

Judaism Welcomes Gentiles

Until about 300 BCE, most people believed that the religion of one's birth was lifelong. For much of the period of the Old Testament, then, Israel did not try to convert other people to the Israelite religion. Israel was to be a light to Gentiles by modeling the way to blessing through the way Israel lived as community.

About 300 BCE this aspect of the social world of the Mediterranean began to change as social mobility became increasingly possible. Many people could choose aspects of their social world, including the religion to which they belonged. Scholars debate whether Judaism became a thoroughgoing missionary religion engaging in large-scale efforts at converting Gentiles, or whether Judaism developed modest strategies for welcoming Gentiles, including rites by which to initiate Gentiles into Judaism.

With the emergence of the end-time anticipation of the realm of God following 300 BCE, some Jewish people believed that God would save Gentiles from the final condemnation and welcome them into the realm. This way of thinking became the seedbed for conception of the nature and purpose of the church in most communities of the New Testament.

Church as Community of the Realm

Most of the New Testament assumed that the realm would come soon, along with the end of the present world and the final judgment. The early church saw Jesus as God's agent, to call people to repent in preparation for the apocalypse, and to live in the present as if the future realm is here. Many churches welcomed Gentiles without asking the Gentiles to be fully initiated into Judaism, since the churches expected the end to come quickly. The first generations of Jesus' followers regarded the church as a group within or closely related to Judaism. Jewish people who shared the view that Jesus was God's agent did not see themselves as rejecting one religion and taking up another, but as embracing a particular form of end-time Judaism.

The New Testament contains several different words for the church. I mention only some representative ones. Each of these images presupposes that God called the church to alert others to the fact of the end-time and to be a community witnessing to the realm.

Church. When the Old Testament was translated from Hebrew into Greek (about 250 BCE), the scholars used the word "church" to translate a Hebrew word for assembly or congregation (as in Deut. 4:10; Neh. 5:13; 2 Chr. 1:3; Mic. 2:5). To be sure, at the time of the New Testament the word "church" was also associated with assemblies in the political world and with trade guilds. But the use of the word "church" signals that communities of Jesus' followers were part of the congregation of Israel.

The body of Christ. Paul frequently refers to the church as the body of Christ. People in the ancient world often used the image of the body to speak of a particular social group. Furthermore, the human body represented the social group and even the universe. The resurrected Christ is the firstborn into the realm. To call the church the body of Christ is to affirm that the church embodies the reality of the realm. As the human body has many distinct parts, so the church has multiple parts, all of which are necessary for the body to carry out its purpose of demonstrating the realm for the sake of people living in the present (1 Cor. 12; Rom. 12:1–8).

Missionary community. The first three Gospels all indicate that the mission of the church includes missionary outreach inviting Gentiles to become part of the community of the realm (Mark 13:10; Matt. 28:19; Luke 24:44–47; Acts 1:6–8). By coming into the church, Gentiles experience a foretaste of the realm and prepare for the apocalypse.

Light of the world. Matthew says that the purpose of the church is to be a light to the world (Matt. 5:14–16). Matthew's church is a part of

Judaism, lighting the world of the first century CE in a way similar to how Isaiah pictured Israel (Isa. 42:6).

Exiles: living between two worlds. First Peter 1:1 describes the church as a community of exiles (cf. 1 Pet. 1:17; 2:11). The church does not belong fully to the present world, nor will they fully be citizens of the realm until the second coming. Now they are to live peacefully within present society to signal Gentiles that the Christian movement is not threatening, while embodying the realm in the church. This community continues the work of Israel as "a chosen race, a royal priesthood, . . . God's own people" (1 Pet. 2:9).

Prophetic community. The book of Revelation pictures the church as a prophetic community that criticizes the Roman Empire for being the embodiment of Satan (e.g., Rev. 13:1–8). The church was to resist the Empire even in the face of imprisonment and martyrdom (e.g., Rev. 1:9–11; 6:9–11; 13:10). The book of Revelation interprets the collapse of the Roman Empire as the judgment of God and encourages the congregation to endure difficulty as they await the second coming (e.g., Rev. 1:7–9, 13:10; 14:12).

Sphere of Heaven on Earth/Way to Heaven Above

In the broad sense, for John the church is to manifest the presence of God within the world and a doorway to eternal life (John 14:1–6). This mission has two dimensions: First, the church is to maintain its own identity as distinct from conventional synagogues and from the world (e.g., John 15:15, 18 to 16:4a; 17:6–19). The members of the congregation are to love one another in the same way that God loves the world and that Jesus loves them (John 13:31–35; 14:15–24; 15:1–17). They are to maintain unity in the face of opposition (John 17). The community is to maintain a sectarian identity.

Second, although John does not say a lot about the community's mission in and to the world, the Johannine Jesus does pray, "As you [God] have sent me into the world, so I have sent them into the world" (John 17:18; cf. 15:16; 20:21). The Holy Spirit empowers the community (John 16:4b-15; 20:22). Jesus revealed God so that those who came to recognize God through Jesus received life in the present and the promise of eternal

life with God (John 3:17; 4:34; 5:36; 10:36; 14:24; 17:3, 8). After Jesus'
ascension, the Johannine congregation is to continue to point to Jesus as
the revelation of God so that people outside the community can believe in
Jesus and thereby receive life now and in heaven (John 20:30–31). Indeed,
the community will do greater works than Jesus (John 14:12). Still, John
is not clear whether the community is to go only to Jewish people or
whether they are to go also to Gentiles to offer life in Jesus' name.

UNDERSTANDINGS OF THE CHURCH
IN CHRISTIAN HISTORY

Themes from the Bible return in the tradition of the church. At the
close of the biblical period the church was a minority community. However, the church grew, and in the fourth century CE became the official
religion of the Roman Empire. From then on, the relationship of the
church to the larger world became a central topic for the church.[2]

Traits Shared by Nearly All Churches in History

Most churches from the end of the biblical period into the contemporary world share two traits. The first relates to identity. Virtually all
churches believe that God has called them into existence. The second
trait is really a combination of practices that many churches carry out—
baptism, worship, breaking the bread and drinking the cup, preaching
and teaching, providing pastoral care, performing marriages and bury-
ing the dead, and providing for the material needs of members of the
congregation and others.

Each church, however, has its own particular understanding of its
nature and purpose. Consequently, the reasons that churches engage in
the practices just named vary. To the casual observer, churches might
appear to be very similar, whereas they can be quite different in under-
lying beliefs about God and their own calls and purposes.

The Makeup of the Church: Predestination or Free Will

Churches have often differed as to whether God predestined people for
salvation or whether individuals had the choice to decide for or against

being saved. This discussion is complicated, and I can only touch on its popular forms. According to the general notion of predestination, God chose certain people for salvation. Although Christians today often object that the notion of predestination is arbitrary toward those who are not selected for salvation, this doctrine intended to emphasize that salvation is absolutely a work of grace. This doctrine offers pastoral assurance to those who are predestined for salvation. Many who hold this position are amazed that God has chosen to save anyone. A church believing in predestination is to help members embrace their election and to live as an elect people until the second coming.

In the case of free will, God as an act of grace saves those who have faith. In the purest form of this understanding, all people are free to choose whether to respond in faith to God's gracious offer of salvation or to reject it. The great danger of this position is that its advocates can effectively regard faith as a work that the believer must perform in order to be saved. A purpose of the free-will church is to awaken people to the need to choose to be either saved or condemned.

Church as Ark to Prepare the Soul for the Journey to Heaven

Many Christians, from the end of the biblical period through today, believe that the fundamental purpose of the church is to prepare people for salvation. From this perspective, preachers have sometimes referred to the church as the ark of salvation, for it carries people through the flood of life and lands them in heaven. The soul can leave the body and go to heaven (or to purgatory and thence to heaven). This church carries out its practices to prepare people to be saved. The purpose of teaching, for instance, is to guide the community in ways of believing and acting that will carry the believer to salvation.

Churches that embrace this view have sometimes held to a popular saying: "There is no salvation outside the church." According to this saying, people must become Christians through the church to be saved. Those who are not a part of the church will not be saved. Other Christians objected that this viewpoint limits God's love and power, and that it undermines the notion of God's grace by turning church membership into a work that we must perform in order to be saved. Still other Christians hold that the notion of salvation as going to heaven is itself too limited, and that salvation must include psychological, relational, and material dimensions of life in the present.

Church as Chaplain to the Dominant Culture

After Christianity became the official religion of the Roman Empire, the church became ever more closely aligned with Western culture. That relationship persisted in strong ways into the Reformation and beyond. In addition to being an ark for individual salvation, the church helped shape social and political life (and the social and political life of the larger world helped shape the church). At times, the life of the church came very close to being the culture of a particular social group, but much of the time the church was more like a chaplain, playing a key advisory role and having considerable power, but also sharing power with others, such as the leaders of the political government. Indeed, the church closely aligned with culture has sometimes been called on to bless the culture, and to educate children and young people so that they will become better citizens who contribute in worthwhile ways to the larger social world.

On the one hand, advocates of this position point out that by being closely aligned with culture, the church has had an opportunity to affect the culture and its values and behaviors. Indeed, at times the church served as the conscience of the culture. On other hand, opponents point out that the values of the church can too easily be compromised by close association with culture. At certain moments the church has simply mirrored prevailing attitudes that were contrary to some of the church's deepest values.

Church as Alternative Social Order

During and after the Reformation (the sixteenth century) some churches believed that the larger culture (including political governments and the churches cooperating with that culture) was so compromised that, to be faithful, believers needed to separate themselves from the larger world and to live separately. These churches functioned as alternative social orders. The Anabaptist movement, for instance, gave birth to communities such as the Mennonites, the Church of the Brethren, the Amish, and other bodies who share this view. Many such Christians participated as little as possible in government-sponsored activities (such as bearing arms and the civil court system), while living as fully as possible according to their interpretations of Christian faith. The purpose of such churches was to help people grasp the corruption of the larger culture and the importance of maintaining a faithful life, and to provide the support necessary for living as an alternative social world.

Some churches have largely felt at home in the culture but have objected to selected aspects of the larger world. In the United States in the first half of the nineteenth century, for example, some churches participated in mainstream culture but objected to slavery. During the First World War, occasional ministers and congregations identified with dominant cultural values but objected to war.

UNDERSTANDINGS OF THE CHURCH
IN CONTEMPORARY COMMUNITIES

As we have noted so often, motifs that appeared in the Bible and in the history of the church recur in the contemporary era. The pluralism in understanding sketched below helps explain why some churches can cooperate so easily on many things (when they share general perceptions of their purposes) and why some churches have difficulty trying to work with one another (they understand their purposes differently). Again, many of these ideas overlap.

Church as Doorway to Heaven

The term "ark of salvation" has almost disappeared from the church, but quite a few churches continue to think of themselves performing that function. I recently heard a minister of such a church describe the congregation by speaking of that congregation as a doorway to heaven. This church prepares people for salvation. Churches in this camp often see evangelistic ministry—converting the unconverted—as fundamental to their purpose. The following incident reveals this attitude. When I was a student in seminary, but on a break in my hometown, I visited a beloved older member of the congregation who admonished me to spend as much time on the last two paragraphs of my sermon as I did on all the rest of the sermon. Why? Because in our church, the sermon ended with an invitation to discipleship, and she averred, "That two minutes is the most important time in the whole service, because that is when people decide whether to come forward and make a confession of faith."

Church as Waiting Room for the Second Coming of Jesus

As noted earlier, while many Christians in history tended to believe in the second coming, they tended to keep that belief in the background. But the notion of preparing for the second coming as the church's first order of business became rather prominent about midway through the nineteenth century and has continued into the present. A large number of Christians today actively anticipate the second coming as a physical event, and believe that the purpose of the church is to alert people to Jesus' return and to help people prepare accordingly.

Some of these churches believe that they can read the signs of the times and ascertain approximately how near we are to the apocalypse. Others are less concerned about locating where we are on the time line, but stress the importance of preparedness. In addition to maintaining personal holiness, some of these churches stress the importance of preparing by doing what Jesus commands, such as feeding the hungry.

Church as Chaplain of Culture

Many churches of European origin continue today to serve as chaplains of the dominant culture in North America by blessing that culture. Some congregations help people make their way through aspects of the Eurocentric way of life in North America that are contrary to God's purposes without challenging the systems, values, and practices that disrupt God's aims. I once heard a minister of such a congregation describe their mission as "patching people up so they can make it from day to day."

At their best, such churches stand for a democratic society of freedom, equality, justice, opportunity, and material resources for all. At less than their best, such congregations foster attitudes and actions that run against the grain of the historic core of Christian teaching. They sometimes pass the hand of blessing over idolatrous forms of nationalism, intolerance, economic exploitation, sexism, racism, classism, and many more self-serving (and other-excluding) modes of behavior. They sometimes believe that their mission includes getting control of government agencies to make those instrumentalities conform more fully to their interpretation of God's purposes.

Church as Community of Self-Care

Few churches would say formally that their primary (or even sole) mission is to care for their own members (to the exclusion of those outside), but occasional congregations function in much that way. Indeed, some congregations are effectively clubs that serve the interests of the existing members, to such an extent that persons attempting to become a part of the social world of the congregation find it very difficult to enter it.

Church Transforming the Social World through Direct Engagement

A number of congregations seek to transform the social world by directly engaging that world. Some congregations believe that God has called them to resist arbitrary forces that oppress human beings and nature, such as racism, sexism, economic exploitation, ageism, militarism, classism, heterosexism, handicappism, nationalism, transnational corporations, and environmental abuse.[3] Indeed such churches sometimes describe a part of their mission with the one word "Resistance."

These communities typically believe that God called them to be positive, active agents of liberating individuals and communities. Liberation churches concentrate on both personal circumstances of oppression and systemic forces that oppress. For example, such a congregation might run a soup kitchen but also engage in activism that would lead to a living wage for farmworkers and the redistribution of land. These congregations seek to liberate the oppressed and to confront the oppressor. The best liberation churches seek to liberate the oppressor, whose life is often repressed by the act of oppressing.

Liberation churches often engage in programs that will strengthen individuals for living in more liberated ways while also working publicly to change oppressive systems. These congregations may cooperate with other organizations who are part of the struggle for liberation.

Strangers and Exiles: Alternative Social World

In some Christian circles today it is popular to speak of the church as a community of strangers or exiles, meaning that the values and behaviors of the church should be different from those of the mainstream culture. The Anabaptist churches discussed in the preceding section continue this mission. In addition, growing numbers of leaders in other historic churches long associated with the mainstream of culture are coming to embrace this aspect of the Anabaptist tradition.

These churches attempt to live according to the social vision of the realm of God. The internal life of the community is to model the realm for the rest of the world. The leadership of the congregation seeks to help the congregation identify and join realm moments and movements.

With regard to external witness, these congregations believe that God has called them to alert the rest of the world to the presence of the realm and to respond accordingly. They sometimes engage the world directly to effect change, but at other times they make a witness in the world that embodies what they see as God's concern for a particular situation without directly pressing for change in the larger social world. These churches sometimes call people and groups in the larger world to repent of personal, corporate, and systemic behaviors that deny the realm.

Four Characteristics of the Church: One, Holy, Catholic, Apostolic

Scholars often point out that Christians have thought of four marks as characteristics of the church: it is one, holy, catholic, and apostolic. At the same time, the church is made up of many different branches, denominations, and movements. How do these four marks relate to the diverse church of today? At various times, saying that the church is *one* meant that it was to be one single institution. Most Christian leaders now, however, think of oneness more in terms of sharing core characteristics and purposes, recognizing that churches express those qualities in different ways. The word *holy* means "perfectly righteous, a thing set apart." The church is to be holy because God has set it apart from other institutions to witness to God's purposes for the world. When saying the church is *catholic* (with a small "c") the intent is that the church is universal (the meaning of catholic), in that the elements of the church are all connected; the individual congregation is not simply an autonomous body, but is part of the larger (and one) church. The church is *apostolic* when it carries forward the faith of the apostles.

QUESTIONS FOR DISCUSSION

1. Recalling the notion of embedded faith in chapter 1, what is your embedded understanding of what the church is called to be and do?
2. Has this chapter prompted fresh thoughts or questions about what you think the church is called to be and do?
3. We can cluster interpretations of the church into five main categories. What do you see as the most positive qualities of each category below? What are your questions about each one?
   a. Doorway to heaven (ark of salvation)
   b. Waiting room for the second coming
   c. Chaplain to the culture
   d. Transforming the culture
   e. Strangers and exiles: alternative social order
4. Take a look at the opening paragraph of this chapter. Which understanding of the church is presupposed by each different proposal being put before the finance team?
5. Sketch your own developing understanding of what God calls the church to be and do (drawing, if useful, on material in this chapter). Please explain why you came to this conclusion.
6. Compare and contrast your understanding of the nature and purpose of the church with how the congregation and denomination or movement to which you belong understands these things.
7. Moving beyond a general statement of the nature and purpose of the church, what do you believe God is calling the congregation to which you belong to be and do? What is the specific purpose of your congregation?
8. Do you believe that people must be a part of the church to experience the fullness of God's blessing, whether you think of that blessing as going to heaven (after death) or coming in the form of experience in the present world?

8
Evil

The Christian community often struggles with how to understand the relationship of the love of God and the existence of evil. When I was serving as cominister of a congregation, one of the most agonizing questions put to me was, "Why do I suffer so much?" People ask this question when confronted by situations such as illness, natural disaster, and personal and social collapse. The Christian tradition contains several different responses.

The church has often said that God is at the same time all-powerful, all-loving, and all-just. At the same time, the church is vexed by the presence of evil in the natural world and in human life. This network of issues is enormously complicated and involves questions that go beyond "Why am I suffering?"

—What is the origin of evil?
—Why do evil things happen?
—What is the relationship of God to evil? Does God cause evil? Does God permit it? What does and will God do about evil?
—What is the role of human beings in evil?
—Why do evil people sometimes prosper?
—Why do natural disaster and sickness take place?
—Are there distinct beings in the world (such as the devil) who do evil things?
—What is the relationship of evil and sin?

To these questions we add the most difficult one that Christian faith faces.

— Why do the innocent suffer?

In thinking about these matters, the church sometimes makes a distinction between the evil that occurs as a result of human behavior (often called moral evil) and the evil that occurs in nature, usually as the result of impersonal forces (frequently referred to as natural evil, evil in nature, physical evil). While the two can be related, it is often helpful to distinguish them. Furthermore, Christians frequently tie together issues of suffering and evil. This chapter can give only passing attention to that relationship.

UNDERSTANDINGS OF EVIL IN THE BIBLE

As noted in chapter 2, many people in the world of the Bible regarded God as all-powerful, that is, able to control all things. Things happened in the world because God directly initiated them or because God permitted them. This distinction comes into play in the discussion of evil. God sometimes caused bad things to happen, but sometimes God allowed bad things to happen either for a specific purpose or, more generally, because the world is broken (see below). Christians sometimes think that the Bible tells a single story of the origin and function of evil, but the Bible contains more than one understanding of evil.

God Pronounced a General Curse on the World in Response to Human Disobedience

According to Genesis 1 and 2, God created the world as a paradise in which all elements of creation lived together in a community of mutual support. The first couple had but one limitation: God commanded that the couple not eat of the tree of the knowledge of good and evil (Gen. 2:16–17). They would die if they ate from the tree.

In Genesis 3, a serpent persuaded Eve to eat from the forbidden tree by promising that her eyes would be opened, she would be like God, and she would not die (Gen. 3:1–5).[1] The first human pair ate the forbidden fruit, disobeying God. Although Christian commentators have sometimes attributed this unfortunate decision to Eve, the text is clear that both the male and the female were responsible. This event is often called the fall (although that designation does not appear in the Bible).

As a consequence, God cursed the snake by taking away the snake's legs and making it crawl. God cursed the woman by increasing her pain in childbearing and by putting her under the rule of her husband. God cursed the male by making his labor burdensome and by ending every human life with death. God cursed the earth (Gen. 3:17–19). The curse does not completely destroy life, but henceforward life in the world only partially represents God's purposes. Both human life and the natural world are now broken.

This story is a way of explaining why the world is fractured. The world is broken because of disobedience. Moral evil results from human beings continuing to act like Adam and Eve, making choices that violate God's purposes. God sometimes has used natural disaster, sickness, and other calamities to punish communities (see the next section). Some people in the biblical period regarded natural evil as the result of the brokenness of the created world. A seasonal flood, for instance, did not indicate divine displeasure with a community's sin, but was a continuing manifestation of the brokenness of creation.

Human Disobedience Brings About Curse in Particular Cases

Deuteronomy is more pointed. God graciously made the covenant with Israel. God provided the commandments as guides for living. When the community obeyed the commandments, blessing resulted in human circumstances and also in nature. When the community disobeyed, then God cursed the people. Natural dysfunction and disaster can be part of the curse (Deut. 27–28). Human behavior and the actions of nature were related. Faithful or unfaithful human actions would lead to nature's being supportive or destructive.

From this point of view, if one lived a blessed life, that would appear to indicate that that person was obedient. If one lived in a state of curse, that would appear to be evidence that one had been disobedient. If one appeared to be obedient, but lived under conditions associated with curse, then one had committed a sin that God saw even if the human eye could not. This latter phenomenon is sometimes called secret or hidden sin.

God sometimes caused people to suffer when they stood in the way of God's purposes. For example, God drowned the army of Pharaoh in the Red Sea (Exod. 14:26–28).

This way of understanding evil explains many cases of evil, especially those resulting from human choices. Furthermore, human beings can abuse the environment, contributing to conditions that lead to disaster in nature. Not everyone in the biblical world subscribed to this view. The book of Job is the most famous biblical objection to the above paradigm. To reduce a long and involved story to a point relevant to the present discussion, the book of Job demonstrates that some suffering does not result from human choices or misconduct. The book of Job does not posit a comprehensive understanding of evil, but it does demonstrate that suffering does not necessarily indicate that the sufferer has sinned.

Satan, the Demons and the Powers

Satan appears a few times in the Old Testament, but always as a functionary in God's court (e.g., Job 1:6–12). Jewish writers began to speak of Satan as an adversary of God only after most of the Old Testament was written. Jewish communities in this period (300 BCE–200 CE) were repeatedly rocked by invasion, national destruction, and occupation by other nations. Sickness, injustice, and violence were intense, and death seemed the greatest affront to God's purposes.

To account for such massive evil, Jewish thinkers concluded that the universe contained Satan, a fallen angel, who sought to wrestle the world away from God. Satan had associates called demons. The principalities and powers were created entities that had taken up with Satan to interrupt God's purposes.

The writers of the New Testament believed that Satan and associates directly challenged God's rule. Satan tried to tempt people away from God's purposes in Jesus. Satan and the demons also worked through nature and could control individuals and communities. According to the book of Revelation, the Roman Empire was a tool of Satan, and when God destroyed the Empire, many people would suffer (Rev. 18; 19).

The presence of Satan did not excuse believers from making faithful choices in the moral sphere. The followers of Jesus were to resist temptation by Satan as Jesus had (Matt. 4:1–11; Mark 1:12–13; Luke

4:1–13) and to endure in the face of difficulty (e.g., Luke 21:19; Col. 1:11; Rev. 13:10). The writers of the New Testament speak little about natural disaster, though several writers see such disasters as signs of the impending apocalypse (e.g., Matt. 24:3–8; Mark 13:4–8; Luke 21:9–11).

Evil Results from Idolatry

Some Jewish thinkers regarded idolatry as the fundamental sin and as a prime cause of moral evil in the world. For example, The Wisdom of Solomon (written possibly about 35 BCE) says, "The idea of making idols was the beginning of fornication, and the invention of them was the corruption of life; for they did not exist from the beginning, nor will they last forever" (Wis. 14:12–13; cf. Wis. 13–15). Idolatry results not only in personal moral failure but in the breakdown of commu-nity (Wis. 14:15–31). While the apostle Paul recognizes the existence of Satan and the demons (e.g., 1 Cor. 8:5), Paul also resonates with idolatry as a cause of moral evil. "[Idolaters] exchanged the glory of the immortal God for images resembling a mortal human being or birds or four-footed animals or reptiles." As a result, "God gave them up in the lusts of their hearts to impurity, to the degrading of their bodies among themselves" (Rom. 1:23–24). For Paul, the moral evil resulting from idolatry and causing social disruption is itself punishment for idolatry.

Suffering That Serves God's Purposes

Biblical writers often think of suffering as against God's purposes. How-ever, there are at least four cases in which the response of an individual or community to certain kinds of suffering can serve God's purposes. For one, when Israel was unfaithful, God punished Israel in order to prompt Israel to repent and change its behavior so that its people could resume the life of blessing (e.g., Joel 1:2–20). Second, remaining faith-ful to God in the midst of suffering can make a witness to others. Isaiah 53, for instance, pictures Israel as God's servant who remains faithful even when made to suffer by God's enemies. Such faithfulness testifies that God can be trusted even in the midst of difficulty. As we noted previously, this interpretation is a seedbed for one of the early inter-pretations of the death of Jesus. Third, some texts view the death of

Jesus as suffering with redemptive consequences (e.g., Rom. 3:24–26).[2] Fourth, suffering can be a form of education (e.g., Heb. 5:8). As we note below, some contemporary Christians are deeply troubled by aspects of this perspective on suffering.

UNDERSTANDINGS OF EVIL IN THE HISTORY OF THE CHURCH

Although the main interpretations of evil from the biblical period continue in the history of the church, some distinctive new viewpoints appear.

Satan Continues to Disrupt Creation

Many Christians continued to believe that Satan is a personal being who is present in the world to oppose God.[3] Christians sometimes believed that Satan continued to supervise an armada of demons who spread evil. In many quarters Christians developed pictures of the devil. The Bible itself does not give a physical description of Satan, but by the Middle Ages many in the church pictured the devil as having horns, and sometimes a tail, carrying a pitchfork.[4] Regardless of how Satan was pictured, many Christians attributed much of the evil in the world to Satan, especially as Satan tempts people to be unfaithful. Martin Luther, for instance, experienced the world as a battleground in which Satan was continuously and aggressively at war with humankind. Indeed, in one famous incident when the devil confronted Luther, the reformer threw an inkwell at the devil.

Some Christians are surprised to learn that occasionally leaders of the church prayed for the devil, believing that the devil would have the opportunity to repent and be saved. A few Christians influenced by universalism (the idea that every human being and entity will be saved) anticipate that Satan will be saved.

The Possibility of Choosing Evil Is Necessary for Growth

Although Irenaeus (ca. 130–200 CE) did not articulate a complete theory of evil, this ancestor in the faith set forth ideas that became the foundation for an approach to evil articulated by John Hick in the contemporary era. According to Irenaeus, the fall (as described by Augustine) never took place, because God never intended to create a perfect paradise. People were made as incomplete creatures who had free choice and, consequently, the potential to grow.

People could mature only by making choices between good and evil. In choosing good, we grow more fully into the likeness of God. The possibility of human beings' choosing evil is *necessary* for human beings to learn and grow. Without the possibility of choosing evil, human freedom of choice would be meaningless. If God did not allow the possibility of evil, then God would compromise human freedom. While God does not directly cause evil, God is responsible for it because God created an imperfect world.

Irenaeus's perspective focuses largely on moral evil. Evil in the social world results from bad choices. But if human beings learn from those choices, they can move toward perfection. In a peculiar way, then, the possibility of disobedience and moral evil serves a good purpose. Irenaeus does not deal so much with the origin of evil in nature. When such evil occurs, however, it can serve God's purposes, for it provides human beings with the opportunity to choose how to respond.

With respect to the question of God's ultimate purposes (chapter 6), Irenaeus believed that at death those who had grown into the likeness of God would go directly to God in heaven. Others would continue the journey of the soul after death until that time when all would be in the presence of God.

Evil Is the Absence of the Good

A provocative chapter in the interpretation of evil was initially voiced by the well-known church writer Augustine (354–430 CE). Unlike Irenaeus, Augustine thought God planned for the world to be altogether good. God did not think that human beings *needed* the possibility of moral evil to develop into the people God wanted them to be. Still, God did create human beings with free choice. A small group of angels rebelled against God and tempted Adam and Eve to want to become like God. Based on this scheme, Augustine popularized the idea of the "fall," which occurred when the first couple abused their freedom by succumbing to the temptation offered by the fallen angels.

For Augustine, then, evil is not a direct power in the world, but a result of the "privation of the good." The evil that continued after the fall was not spurred by an actual entity (such as the devil) but resulted from the absence of the good in the same way that absence of light is the essence of darkness. The darkness does not have physical power.

Since the fall, moral evil has resulted from the misuse of freedom by human beings. They fail to act for the good. Evil in the natural world was God's punishment for human beings' falling to temptation.

Whereas Irenaeus viewed God as responsible for evil by requiring the possibility that human beings could choose evil in order to develop, Augustine did not hold God responsible for evil, for God made the creation free of evil. The misuse of freedom is responsible for evil. Augustine anticipated a final judgment at the end of history, at which time those who have used their freedom properly would enter heaven, but those who abused it would be punished in hell. After that, God will restore the world to its original perfect state (which does not include evil).

Evil Is an Illusion

A few people throughout history have argued that evil does not have any objective reality but is only an illusion. For such folk, everything is good, even if human beings cannot always recognize this fact. The philosopher Spinoza (1632–1677) contended that we make the mistake of thinking that evil is real because we human beings measure things only in relationship to ourselves and do not consider the big picture of life. In the bigger picture, things (including circumstances that we evaluate as evil) may have values that we cannot see from our limited perspective. Another philosopher (Leibniz, 1646–1716) reinforced this view by contending that the present world must be the best of all possible worlds because God (who is perfect) could not have made any other kind of world. From the point of view of public recognition, the most well-known exponent of this point of view was Mary Baker Eddy (1821–1910), founder of Christian Science. To her, sickness seems real because the human mind errs in believing it is real. Evil has no real power.

Suffering That Serves God's Purposes

In history, the church continues the same four notions of certain kinds of suffering serving God's purposes that were present in the biblical period, though one of them is expanded. Some people continue to believe that God punishes sin by sending evil circumstances, with God often hoping that people will repent. Many believe that remaining faithful to God in difficult circumstances testifies to God's trustworthiness. The most noteworthy development in the history of the church is the expansion of interpretations of the horrific death of Christ as an event that serves God's purposes. For example, church leaders vastly enlarge their analysis of the foundation and function of the theory of the crucifixion of Christ as substitutionary atonement, Christ having suffered for human beings in order to pay for their sins. From the perspective of penal substitution (a form of substitutionary atonement), God punished Christ instead of punishing us. In either case, God demanded the suffering of Christ in order to fulfill the demands of justice. Some people continue to think of suffering as a mode of education.

UNDERSTANDINGS OF EVIL
IN THE CONTEMPORARY CHURCH

The preceding viewpoints continue in the contemporary church, and others are added to them. These viewpoints all account for evil that results from human choice, but some of them have more difficulty explaining sickness and other evils in nature.

Satan Disrupts the Creation

A number of congregations and Christians believe that Satan and the demons are personal entities who are in the world. Although few people (if any) believe that Satan has horns and a twitching tail, many do think that Satan is present to tempt individuals and communities and to disrupt human life and the world in other ways. This way of thinking accounts for both moral evil and evil in nature. My impression is that most people who believe in Satan as an actual being also believe in a sovereign and all-powerful God. They often struggle to explain why such a God continues to allow Satan and the demons to exercise such brutal power in the human community and in the natural world. Occasionally I get the further impression that some people use this perception as a way of excusing themselves (or others) for responsibility in situations in which human decisions have resulted in evil by saying, "The devil made me do it."

God Gives People a Cross to Bear

Some people view difficult circumstances—such as illness, or living with a difficult child—as their cross to bear. These Christians seem to think that just as God sent Jesus to the cross, so God has given them some form of suffering to endure. Indeed, a common saying is "God never gives you more than you can bear." Moreover, they seldom notice that the cross of Jesus and the kinds of difficulties they have in mind are usually quite different. Jesus voluntarily accepted the cross for the benefit of the world. Church members usually have in mind suffering that results from sickness or other evils in nature or from actions that other people take, rather than their own decisions to act for the good of others. People who follow this train of thought sometimes think that God seeks to teach them a lesson through suffering. But often such folk seem puzzled as to the purpose of their suffering.

Evil Is the Absence of Good

In Bible-study groups I sometimes hear participants state that they regard evil as the absence of good. They regard the experience of suffering as real, but that suffering is caused not by an active power that seeks to harm them but by people not acting on the good. As someone said, "When you don't do right, you turn the situation over to the wrong." This way of thinking can explain moral evil. But my impression is that laity who hold this view seldom consciously follow the fullness of thinking represented by Augustine (above) and are uncertain about how it relates to evil in nature. More than once I have asked such a person how that person accounts for physical evil, only to receive the response of a puzzled look and an uncomfortable silence. Augustine, of course, would say that evil in nature is a lingering result of the fall.

The World Is Broken

In a motif reminiscent of Augustine—that evil in the spheres of both morality and nature is a lingering result of the fall—some Christians today do not try to explain the origin of evil, but believe that evil in nature is simply an expression of the fact that the world is broken and is not the kind of place that God intended it to be. One of my teachers described evil as "a madness in the world," recognizing that moral evil results from human decisions and attributing illness and natural disaster and tragedies to the brokenness of the world.

God Sends Evil to Punish Sin

Occasionally I read or hear that God sends evil to punish sin. For example, when my spouse and I served a congregation in Nebraska, a series of tornados blasted through our city, destroying homes and taking lives. A local preacher interpreted this event as God's punishment, because our community had a club on the edge of town that featured a topless dancer. Sometimes people think that God sends punishment for the purpose of awakening people to repentance, but at other times people seem to think that God sends punishment as an end in itself. Given the amount and intensity of evil in the world today, according to this viewpoint God should have destroyed the world by now.

We Suffer the Consequences of Our Own Bad Decisions

Many Christians believe that God does not directly punish us, but that evil is the consequence of our own bad decisions. This situation is self-evidently true in the moral sphere. This perspective also illuminates some aspects of evil in nature. Some people who smoke cigarettes develop lung cancer. Human beings abuse nature and wake up to discover that nature is affected adversely. For example, human beings have poured so much heat into the atmosphere that global warming is now threatening to melt significant portions of the polar ice caps and to raise the water level on seacoasts all around the world. Still, poor choices on the part of human beings do not create all sickness or all the evil in nature.

Contemporary Understanding of the Powers
as Systems of Oppression

As noted previously, in the New Testament the language of principalities and powers refers to elements of creation that have lost their
way. Created good, they no longer serve God's purposes. An important movement, especially among clergy, interprets the powers as social
forces that work against God's aims of love and justice for communities. The powers are not personal entities, but are patterns of assumptions, values, and behaviors that repress individuals and communities.
Individuals and communities often go along with such powers without
being aware that the powers distort God's aims. We often take the
powers for granted.

Often the principalities and the powers elevate the social domina-
tion of limited groups at the expense of others. Examples of such powers are racism, sexism, ageism, classism, capitalism, handicappism, and
heterosexism. These powers function as social systems that create brutal
conditions for people who are subject to them. Like the perspective
discussed immediately above (we suffer the consequences of our bad
decisions), this one explains the evil in nature that results from powers
that direct the human community to abuse the environment, but does
not account for all evil in nature.

Evil Is for Our Benefit

John Hick builds on Irenaeus's understanding of evil (above) and
makes even more explicit the idea that the presence of evil leads to
greater goods than we know now.[5] Hick does not accept the view of the
fall as articulated in Augustine, but believes that God authorizes evil for
the sake of prompting the human community to recognize the possibility of a greater good. For example, the distress of adolescence is a part
of the reason that most young people develop into mature adults. The
suffering caused by cancer leads researchers to invent ways of treating
cancer that we do not now possess. People sometimes speak of this process as soul-making, that is, our experiences of evil (in concert with all
of our life experiences) contribute to our personal growth and matur-
ing. From this point of view, God is responsible for evil because the
experience of evil is necessary for growth.

By way of critical reflection, we can see that the experience of evil does sometimes lead to improvement in life, but that is not always the case. Moreover, this experience seems to devalue experiences of suffering in and of themselves. Indeed, this perception regards screams of pain as instruments of the journey to some greater good.

Human Beings and Others Do Not Respond to the Divine Lure

A group of thinkers mentioned several times in this book do not believe that the church can say that God is, at the same time, altogether loving, altogether powerful, altogether just. Evil is a litmus case for this approach. A God who is completely loving, powerful, and just would eliminate evil. The continued presence of evil means that God is limited in one of those three attributes. These thinkers—often called process or relational theologians—contend that God is altogether loving and altogether just, but not altogether powerful. However, God is not powerless. From their point of view, God does not have the power to control evil. Indeed, God acts not through unilateral exercise of force but through lure or persuasion. God is present in every situation seeking to lure people toward the good.

To these Christians, moral evil results from people not responding to the lure of God toward love and justice. Even though God does not desire sickness or evil in nature, God cannot directly control such things. At this point, process thinkers take an unusual tack. They argue that every entity is living. The table on which I am writing this book may appear to be inanimate, but it is made up of atoms that are in constant motion. It is constantly in process and can respond to stimuli. Every entity in the world has freedom. Some entities—such as human beings—have high degrees of consciousness, while others—such as animals, the clouds, and this table—have lower and lower degrees of consciousness. Nevertheless, they are all alive and can respond positively or negatively to the lure toward a world of love and justice. Natural evil results from elements of creation exercising their freedom in ways that are destructive.

Nevertheless, when elements of the world act in ways that frustrate God's purposes, God does not give up on them. On the contrary, according to this perspective, God is present in every moment with every element in creation, seeking to lure the various elements of the world into harmony and mutual support. God cannot singularly create such a world, but God is ever at work to lure elements of the world toward it.

Protest Against Evil

A handful of Christians, led by John Roth, do not so much try to explain evil as to express a protest against it.[6] These Christians accept the traditional notions that God has ultimate control over all things and the ability to do anything that God wants. Consequently, God could alleviate or end suffering. The fact that God does not want to do so must mean that God does not want this to happen. This makes God responsible for evil and for suffering. Given the limitations of human power, the only meaningful human response is to *protest* to God.

Roth sees our understanding of God as key. Like the process theologians above, he also thinks that we cannot believe that God is simultaneously all powerful and all loving. If we follow the process theologians in saying that God is not all powerful, then we are left with a God who cannot change the world very much. Believing in such a God is futile. A God who is not all loving offers the human family more hope. Such a God has the power to change things dramatically *if moved to do so*. Protest—essentially saying to God, "Enough is enough"—is the best way to try to persuade God to do away with evil.

Evil Is an Illusion or a Matter of Perception

Only a few Christians today think that evil is an illusion. But a handful do believe that we interpret evil as a bad thing only because we do not have the perspective to see how events that we describe as evil fit into the larger picture. Such folks seem not to recognize that while particular occasions of evil spark people to respond by making decisions and discoveries that lead to good, that does not take away from the difficulty and suffering of particular circumstances.

Suffering That Serves God Purposes

The four forms of suffering that serve God's purposes identified in a previous section occur again in the contemporary church.

QUESTIONS FOR DISCUSSION

1. Recalling the notion of embedded faith in chapter 1, what is your embedded understanding of the origin and extent of evil?
2. Has this chapter prompted fresh thoughts or questions about what you have thought about evil and God's relationship to it?
3. Which of the understandings of evil set forward in this chapter do you find more and which less compelling? What makes them so? How would you express your own understanding of evil in dialogue with these possibilities?
4. Imagine that you are making a call on a member of your congregation who is in the hospital with a terminal illness. The patient asks, "Why did God do this to me?" Given your understanding of evil, how do you respond?
5. Thinking back to chapter 6 ("God's Ultimate Purposes"), what do you believe God is now doing and will ultimately do about evil?
6. What would you say to a friend who has suffered a tragedy and asks you, "Why has this terrible thing happened to me?"

9
Christianity and Other Religions

Only two generations ago, on a day-to-day basis Christians in the United States largely came into contact with people who were at least nominally Christian or Jewish. Indeed, these people sometimes said, "We are a Christian nation." Of course, people who belong to other religions have long lived in North America, but Christians who moved in the mainstream of Eurocentric culture did not often see them. As I grew up in a Christian-majority small town on the edge of the Ozark Mountains, for instance, I seldom ran into people who belonged to other religions. I did not have a serious conversation about religion with a Jewish person until I was a student at Union Theological Seminary and visited the Jewish Theological Seminary of America across the street. To be sure, in Bible school and in youth group we sometimes pondered what other religions were like and whether people would be saved if they belonged to other religions. Many of us assumed that Christian faith was the normative expression of religion.

Today, however, North America is in a situation of religious plural-ism. Christians, Jewish people, Muslims, Bahais, Hindus, and people of other religions—and no religion at all—live on the same block, work in the same office, shop in the same mall, study in the same classroom, attend the same athletic and artistic events, and serve in the same governmental structures. Churches, synagogues, mosques, temples, and other religious assemblies discuss whether to work together, and if so, how.

What Christians believe about other religions can have direct consequences regarding how Christians relate to adherents of other religions. Do Christians regard other religions as valid? Do we think of them as containing helpful insights, though flawed? Does the church believe that God calls Christians to convert members of other religions to Christianity? The relationship among Christianity, Judaism, and Islam occupies a special place in this discussion because all three of these religions come from the God of Sarah and Abraham.

OTHER RELIGIONS AND THE PEOPLE OF THE BIBLE

For much of the period of the Old Testament, the relationship of different religions took place on a different basis than it does now. In those days, people did not have a separation of religion and state. Religion was not a separate part of life. Rather, religious identity was usually associated with tribal or national identity. People tended to be born into a religion and to live in it all their lives. Beginning about 300 BCE, people did have more freedom to affiliate voluntarily with religions of their choice.

The Israelites Recognized Other Gods

Christians are sometimes startled to discover that the people of Israel recognized the existence of other gods until about the sixth century BCE. Perhaps the oldest fragment of the Old Testament, Exodus 15:11, asks, "Who is like you, O [God], among the gods?" The First Commandment acknowledges other gods (Exod. 20:3; Deut. 6:13). While other nations had deities, the Israelites tended to believe their God was the most powerful (e.g., 2 Sam. 7:22; Ps. 89:8–9). God was the president of a heavenly council of deities or other heavenly beings (e.g., Deut. 10:17; Ps. 89:8). The problems with Israelites worshiping other gods were that (1) the other deities did not have the pathway to blessing, and (2) they did not have enough power to protect Israel.

Israel Comes to Believe in Only One God

Isaiah (eighth century BCE) sounds the first clear note that Israel should believe that only one God exists. "I am the first and I am the last," God says; "besides me there is no god" (Isa. 44:6). This phenomenon is called monotheism. Other religions had deities, but from Isaiah's point of view, these gods had no real existence. Some Israelite writers lampooned the idols that represented such deities: "Our God is in the heavens. . . . [but the gods of the nations] their idols are silver and gold, the work of human hands. They have mouths, but do not speak; eyes, but do not see. . . . they make no sound in their throats. Those who make them are like them; so are all who trust in them" (Ps. 115:3–8; for an even more scathing critique, see Wis. 14:12–31).

By the time of the New Testament, many Jewish communities acknowledged the existence of suprahuman beings (Satan, demons, principalities and powers). However, Jewish people conceived of these entities not as gods, but as creatures who went amok and who continued to exist only because God permitted them to do so.

The Early Churches as a Group within Judaism

As we have mentioned before, some Christians today think that Jesus came to found Christianity as a new religion. Advocates of this viewpoint often believe that Jesus and the early church viewed Judaism as a defunct religion and replaced it with Christianity. (This idea is often called supersessionism.) However, scholarship in the last forty years has recognized that Jesus never renounced Judaism, but lived as a faithful Jewish believer. He perceived his purpose as announcing the present-but-partial realm of God and urging people to prepare for the final coming of that realm. The first disciples were Jewish. After the resurrection, they lived as a group within Judaism. As the early church grew, it saw itself not as a new religion, but as a manifestation of Judaism whose particular mission was to alert the larger community to the imminence of the end-time and to welcome Gentiles into the church.

After the fall of Jerusalem (70 CE) tensions developed between some conventional synagogues and the early churches, especially regarding whether the churches should welcome Gentiles without requiring complete conversion to Judaism. However, these tensions were in-house, rather like the differences between the church board and a Bible-school class regarding how to use the congregation's mission fund.

Other Religions Contain Some Reliable Guidance

Although condemnation of idolaters is a strong theme in the New Testament, occasional passages indicate that some figures in other religions and philosophical schools did have some authentic insight. In the book of Acts, for instance, Luke pictures Paul preaching to a group of unconverted Gentiles in Athens. In his sermon, Paul quotes approvingly from the Greek philosopher Epimenides: "In him we live and move and have our being." Paul also cites appreciatively the Greek poet Artapanus: "For we too are his offspring" (Acts 17:28). While such non-Jewish sources were trustworthy, their guidance was incomplete. God "commands all people everywhere to repent, because [God] has fixed a day on which [God] will have the world judged in righteousness" (Acts 17:30–31).

Condemnation of Idolaters

In the time of the New Testament, many writers in conventional Judaism and the church condemn idolatry and idolaters. Jewish people and Gentiles who have turned to the God of Israel through Jesus Christ are to avoid idolatry. Paul says flatly that idolaters will not inherit the realm of God (1 Cor. 6:9). The Corinthians should not even associate with idolaters (1 Cor. 5:10; cf. 1 Pet. 4:3). First Enoch (an end-time Jewish book written shortly before the time of Jesus) declares that idolaters will be consigned to eternal punishment (1 En. 99:14). The book of Revelation anticipates that the ultimate destination for idolaters "will be in the lake that burns with fire and sulfur" (Rev. 21:8; 22:15). These writers see no positive values in other religions.

The Early Church Rejects the Religion of the Roman Empire

The writer of the book of Revelation provides the only sustained reflection on a specific other religion in the New Testament. Revelation 13:1–10 pictures a dragon on the seashore supervising a beast emerging from the sea. The dragon is Satan and the beast is the Roman Empire: the Empire is an agent of Satan. The dragon has real power, which is invested in the beast so that the beast can do real damage to communities on the earth. People worship the dragon by worshiping the beast (Rev. 13:4).

Revelation 13:11–18 describes a second beast, which looks like a lamb, but that speaks like the dragon. This second beast is the Roman imperial religion put in place to promote emperor worship and to lead people to regard the Empire as divinely authorized. Roman religion deceived people by imitating the true religion of Israel. Roman priests performed great signs, even making fire come down from heaven, raising the dead, and creating a community whose diversity was similar to that of the church (Rev. 13:12–16). Imperial religion functioned by imitating the real religion (Judaism and its sect, Christianity) and deceiving people. Of course, Romans helped kill those who would not worship the first beast (Rev. 13:15b). Those who follow the beast face eternal condemnation (Rev. 21:8; 22:15).

Salvation Only in Jesus Christ?

In chapter 6 we mentioned that an important issue in today's church is whether the church believed (and can believe today) in limited or universal salvation. An aspect of this discussion is whether one must become a Christian to be saved. Since we focus on that theme in chapter 6, we need not repeat it here. However, most voices in the church have spoken in favor of limited salvation. Furthermore, most such people regard salvation as impossible outside the church. Some folks who do believe in universal salvation believe that God will ultimately make everyone Christian. Some people, however, believe that non-Christians will be welcomed into salvation as non-Christians.

CHRISTIANITY AND OTHER RELIGIONS IN THE HISTORY OF THE CHURCH

A constant factor in the history of the church was the viewpoint that Christianity is *the* true religion. However, as the following survey shows, there were other perspectives.

An Early Tradition Viewing Judaism Positively

Not long ago, many scholars believed that Christianity broke away from Judaism and became a separate religion by the middle or late first century CE. Scholars spoke of a definitive parting of the ways. Many scholars, though, have lately come to think of Judaism and early Christianity as separating more slowly. Many Christians continued to see themselves related to Judaism, perhaps into the early Middle Ages. Christians in these circles regarded Judaism as an honored religion and believed its adherents had full standing before God. I mention this revised view because some Christians believed that the church in history monolithically assumed it was superior to Judaism. In fact, on this subject (as on so many others) Christian viewpoints were more diverse.

The Church Superior as to Other Religions

For the most part, the church has viewed Christianity as superior to other religions. Considerable diversity existed under this umbrella, however. Some Christians thought the church had an exclusive hold on truth and that all other religions were altogether false. Some leaders did think that other religions could contain some genuine religious insight because God visited all people, though, of course, the highest expression of insight was in the Bible and the church. Occasional Christian thinkers thought that other religions stole their insights from Christian sources. Some religions were believed to have originated with Satan. Although today's Christians usually associate the word "crusades" with wars of European Christians against Muslims, some European Christians also engaged in crusades in central Europe aimed to stamp out native religions and to establish Christianity.

Martin Luther (1483–1546), the first of the Protestant Reformers, thought that the saving knowledge of God came only through the church. Other religions had no standing before God. Even if people who belonged to other religions believed in the one God, they would not be saved unless they also accepted Christ.

John Calvin (1509–1564) shared Luther's view that the Christian religion was the highest form of spiritual knowledge. Being a member of the church, however, did not necessarily mean that an individual was saved, for Calvin distinguished between the visible and the invisible church. The invisible church is made up of all those whom God has chosen to save, and its bounds go beyond that of the visible church. The visible church, unfortunately, contains persons who are unfaithful. However, Calvin had a low view of the notion that human beings could come to the knowledge of God through nature. Calvin, in contrast to most other Christian leaders of his period, had a high view of Judaism.

One of the most storied results of this viewpoint was the massive missionary push of churches in Europe (and later in North America) during the seventeenth, eighteenth, nineteenth, and early twentieth centuries. With great commitment, these churches sent thousands of missionaries to other lands to convert non-Christians.

God Revealed a Partial Measure of Truth to Other Peoples

During the sixteenth century, a movement known as humanism believed that many non-Christians possessed genuine (if partial) religious understanding. Some humanists believed that the ideas of the philosophers and poets from antiquity (such as Plato and Aristotle) were consistent with the ideas of the Bible, Christ, and the church. Most Christian humanists did think that Christian understanding was superior to other sources of insight.

Perhaps the most well-known Christian humanist was Erasmus, a well-educated Dutch Roman Catholic scholar (1466?–1536). Erasmus believed that God instilled many of the divine purposes in nature so that individuals could acquire virtue by obeying natural law. The church should respect and learn from the wisdom of non-Christian sources. While Erasmus believed that salvation was possible for enlightened non-Christians, he thought that salvation ordinarily came through the church.

Huldrych Zwingli (1484–1531) believed with Erasmus that while other religions were inferior, God could save non-Christians who manifest qualities of the faithful life. Zwingli came to this conclusion not by following Erasmus on natural revelation, but because Zwingli believed that God had elected to save some people outside the church. As with Calvin, the church was not simply the institution visible in history but was made up of the elect (including non-Christians) from every time and place.

Many Enlightenment Thinkers Recognize Religious Pluralism

The previous viewpoints continue to occur in the same time period as the age of Enlightenment (beginning in the eighteenth century, with effects continuing into today). Under the impetus of the scientific method and corresponding developments in philosophy, many Enlightenment thinkers believed that no religion was altogether the result of direct revelation from God. Because all religions have been influenced by their historical contexts, they all contain elements of relativity. To the Enlightenment mind, truth and error could be found anywhere. Different religions resulted because people could come into contact with the divine in any setting and communities organized the different religions in different ways.

Some thinkers influenced by the Enlightenment believed that the knowledge of God was progressive, evolving in stages, and that Christianity was a more highly evolved form of religion. Some Enlightenment analysts contended that Christian faith was normative for them. For many people, reason became as much a norm for measuring truth as the Bible and Christian tradition, and for some people reason was supreme. The claims of the Bible and Christian doctrine that violated the canons of reason were considered inferior, even superstitious.

The Church in Tension with Judaism and Islam

Because they occupied a large place in Christian consciousness in the history of the church, I mention the church's often tendentious attitude toward both Judaism and Islam. Although we have earlier called attention to the fact that some Jewish and Christian circles continued positive interaction into the early Middle Ages, many Christians came to view Judaism as inferior. Indeed, occasional Christians viewed the Jewish people as children of the devil. At various times, members of the church sought to convert Jewish people voluntarily, to force Jewish people to become Christian, to force Jewish people to live in segregated ghettos, and even to physically persecute Jewish people, including putting some to death. Such thinking contributed significantly to the rise of anti-Semitism. Of course, some Christians lived alongside Jewish people without rancor, and some voices in the church spoke positively about Judaism. John Calvin, for instance, taught respect for the Jewish people.

Islam became a religion under the guidance of the prophet Muhammad (ca. 570–632). Over the history of the church since then, Christians have responded to Islam in two main ways. For one, many Christians viewed Islam almost altogether negatively. When members of Islam moved into Palestine and occupied Jerusalem and other Christian holy sites, the church launched the Crusades, which were intended to wrest control of those places from the hands of Muslims (1095–1291). Christians sometimes massacred the Muslim inhabitants of conquered cities. After the Crusades, many Christians viewed Islam with disdain; at least one Christian leader referred to Islam as a predecessor of the antichrist. For the other way, some Christians in history took more tolerant attitudes toward Islam and even sought to identify elements of belief and practice shared by the two religions. Occasional Christians asserted that the Koran contains some truth. Many Christians in history who sought the conversion of Muslims did so in a context of advocating peaceful coexistence.

CHRISTIANITY AND OTHER RELIGIONS IN THE CONTEMPORARY CHURCH

We may distinguish five major interpretations of the relationship of the church and other religions in the contemporary world.[1] Each viewpoint has distinct implications for how the church should interact with those who belong to other religions.

Christianity Is the Only True Religion

With nuances similar to those we have already encountered among people in the past who believed that Christianity is the only true religion, some Christians today continue in the same path. From this point of view, the other religions are false, and those who follow them cannot know the fullness of God or salvation. The church has little to learn from other religions, and is obligated to expose the falsehood in other religions. These Christians seek to convert participants in other religions to Christianity.

I sometimes hear Christians who subscribe to more inclusive viewpoints (below) assume that Christians who believe that Christianity is the only authentic religion are arrogant and self-righteous. While that may occasionally be true, when reflecting the best of their tradition Christians who subscribe to this view often have a deep concern for those who are not Christian and do not want nonbelievers to be shortchanged in religious experience in this life or to suffer condemnation in the next.

All Religions Are Essentially the Same

Some Christians believe that all religions are essentially the same. This viewpoint can be summed up by statements such as, "The different religions are just different paths to the same goal," or, "We're all climbing the same mountain." Although names for the holy, other aspects of language, personal and community practices, and cultural forms may differ, each religion contains the same essence, the same core. All who practice their own religions will come to the ultimate experience of fulfillment. From this point of view, members of one religion are not called on to convert members of other religions. Instead, members of different religions can discover what the religions have in common and what members of the multiple religions might learn from one another. In the immediate moment, such discoveries should lead to a decrease in hostility among the different religions and their practitioners.

Religions Have Evolved: Different Religions Are at Different Stages

A handful of Christians today think of religions as more and less evolved. All religions contain kernels of truth—and falsehood, with some being more complete than others. Christians with this perception usually envision Christianity as the most complete expression of religion because Jesus Christ is the highest form of revelation, and the church has the Bible as a guide to evaluating the other religions. Judaism and Islam are fairly evolved forms of religion, but not as high as Christianity, since neither confesses Jesus Christ. Asian and African religions tend to be lower in the pyramid of completeness. Christians in this camp look at other religions with respect, since all religions contain some reliable insight. The church needs to understand the contributions of other religions. At the same time, such Christians are motivated to convert people who belong to other religions (and to critique the religions themselves), since they have only partial understanding of the fullness of divine revelation.

Each Religion Has Its Own Integrity: Peaceful Coexistence

An important movement in the last thirty years believes that each religion creates its own view of the world through its language and practices. Each religion creates a distinct culture, has its own integrity, and is to be honored as such. The different religions do not contain a universal essence and are not different versions of the same thing. Nor are the different religions at different evolutionary stages from a common core. Each religion is particular (to use a favorite expression from this movement).

Leading thinkers often speak of language as a game, in the sense that each game has its own rules and those who participate play by the rules of that game. Football, basketball, baseball, and softball, for instance, each involve balls, but the balls are different in each game. The same expression, "Pass me the ball," means something different in each game.

Each religion initiates its followers into a different understanding of the holy, of the goal of the religious life, of what the religion offers and requires, and of the purposes of human life and of the world. The different religions exist alongside one another like different shops in the great mall of human experiences. Most people (in my experience) who think in this vein are Christians, but they do not insist that the Christian religion is hierarchically superior to other religions. Exponents of this way of thinking hope that the different religions can peacefully coexist with one another. Rather than attempt to convert committed people from other religions to Christianity, Christians seek to attain a measure of understanding of those religions. The church is to enact its own values within its own life and in its witness in the larger world. The church can be open to people from other religions (or from no religion) who become interested in Christianity, and can even initiate such folks into the church.

Religions Can Cause One Another to Change

Some Christians who view life as a constant process of change are open to the possibility that Christianity could be changed by encountering other religions, and that other religions could change in response to Christianity. This perception is rooted in the belief that religions are not once-for-all deposits of divine revelation, but are human constructions that arise from the best insights that people have at particular moments.

Changing circumstances can prompt individuals and communities to notice things that they had not previously observed. Christians already know this with respect to their own faith. New contexts with new questions and new needs can prompt the church to see things related to God, Christ, the Spirit, the church, or Christian practice that they had not recognized previously. The same phenomena can occur when Christians come into contact with other religions. They may discover possibilities they had not seen, which may cause the community to think afresh about aspects of its life. In this transformational perspective, the church offers its interpretations to others while listening to the perspectives of others with an ear open for what the church may learn from them.

Current Views: Judaism and Islam

While some Christians today continue to believe that Jewish and Muslim people should convert to Christianity, significant numbers of Christians have more positive views of those religions. In the wake of the Holocaust—the murder of six million Jewish people by the Nazis during World War II—many Christian teachers began to think afresh about the relationship of Judaism and Christianity. Many Christians now regard Judaism as a religion with full standing before God. The two religions are not identical, but they do share a common God and many common values. Judaism offers its adherents a life-giving relationship with God through grace revealed through the covenant with Abraham and Sarah and guided by Torah. Christianity offers its adherents a life-giving relationship with God through grace revealed through the covenant made available to Gentiles through Jesus Christ, and guided by a summary of Torah—loving God with heart, mind, soul, and strength and loving our neighbors as ourselves (e.g., Mark 12:28–34; Matt. 22:34–40; Luke 10:25–28). Both seek to witness to God's will for all people to live in peace (*shālōm*), justice, love, and abundance. Christians are not to convert Jewish people to Christianity, but instead the church is called to find joint missions that it can undertake with the synagogue.

Christians are often less familiar with Islam than with Judaism. Moreover, Christian perception is clouded in some quarters by associating Islam with world terrorism. Nevertheless, many Christians follow leading Islamic scholars who contend that the fundamental purpose of Islam is revealed in the fact that the name Islam means submission, and that surrender to God leads to a life of peace with others. The five pillars of Islam are radical monotheism, prayer performed five times a day, charity, fasting during Ramadan (a month in the early fall), and a pilgrimage to Mecca. Islamic law indicates how to put these principles into practice in everyday life. In North America, some Christian congregations are exploring what they have in common with neighborhood mosques and how the two communities—and the local synagogue— might cooperate in mission.

QUESTIONS FOR DISCUSSION

1. Recalling the notion of embedded faith in chapter 1, what is your embedded understanding of the relationship of Christianity and other religions?
2. Has this chapter prompted fresh thoughts or questions about what you have thought concerning Christianity and other religions?
3. We can cluster interpretations of the relationship of Christianity and other religions into five main groups. What do you see as the most positive qualities of each category below? What are your questions about each one?
   a. Christianity is the only true religion: we must evangelize members of other religions.
   b. All religions are essentially the same: Christians and members of other religions should celebrate what we have in common.
   c. Different religions have evolved to different levels, with Christianity reaching the highest level: Christians should respect other religions while being confident in their own beliefs.
   d. Peaceful coexistence among religions that are simply different: Christians should respect the otherness of other religions and engage in dialogue to compare and contrast where we differ and what we have in common; Christians can engage in projects with others on the basis of shared interests.

   e. Religions cause one another to change: Christians should
      be open to the ways that other religions may cause Christi-
      anity to transform itself.
4. Sketch your own developing understanding of the relationship of
   Christianity and other religions. Why do you find this position
   persuasive?
5. Given your understanding of Christianity and other religions,
   how will you act toward other people who belong to other religions?
6. If you can, invite some members of a nearby synagogue and
   mosque to visit your Bible class. Assemble a group of comparable
   representatives from your own class. Convene the three delega-
   tions as a panel. After asking each group to give a five-minute
   summary of the main pillars of their religion, invite each delega-
   tion to describe how their religion perceives a particular topic.
   For example, how does each religion understand sin and forgiveness? What are the central holy days for each religion, and what
   do they mean?

Final Exercise
Formulating a Faith of Your Own

Along the way you have probably been identifying preferences regarding what you would like to believe about each of the categories of belief discussed in this book—God, Jesus Christ, the Holy Spirit, the Trinity, God's ultimate purposes, the church, evil, and Christianity and other religions. This closing section of the book sets out three basic criteria for formulating a faith of your own, and then gives you an opportunity to pull together a comprehensive statement of what you believe, at least for now. You may rethink aspects of your faith again and again in response to new information, fresh insights and perspectives, reconsideration of old ideas, and experiences that cause you to take a second look at what you have thought previously.

If at all possible, your thinking should take place in a community. Members of a small group can often identify strengths and weaknesses in your work that you do not see. They can help you name and build on important ideas, and they can often point out contradictions, gaps, and other weak points that may never occur to you.

FOUR CRITERIA FOR FORMULATING A FAITH

Because the world is finite and sin-stained, we can never have full and complete knowledge of the infinite God. We are always in a situation of reaching for the best interpretation that we can. In this regard, David

Tracy, who taught for many years at the University of Chicago, notes that we can articulate a faith that is adequate.[1] We can never know everything, but we can develop perspectives that are good enough. In a general way, an understanding of Christian faith should satisfy the following four criteria.

A Faith in Continuity with the Core
of the Bible and Christian Tradition

First, a faith should be in recognizable continuity with the core of the Bible and historic Christian tradition. Such a faith should express confidence in God as ultimate reality, show how Jesus Christ is related to God's purposes, point to the empowering presence of the Holy Spirit, describe the church, and express a compelling vision of life for the present and future.

Christian communities can discuss and even debate whether a faith is in "recognizable continuity with the core of the Bible and historic Christian tradition." As a result of such conversation, a believer may not accept some of the claims that are in the Bible and church history. Indeed, some of my deepest convictions insist that I reject some aspects of the biblical witness. For instance, the Bible assumes the validity of slavery, and even admonishes, "Slaves, obey your earthly masters in everything" (Col. 3:22; cf. Eph. 6:5–8; 1 Tim. 6:1–2; Titus 2:9–10; 1 Pet. 2:18–25). Every Christian I know is convinced that God is opposed to slavery. One important reason for being opposed to slavery is that it goes against the Bible's own picture of God as loving, compassionate, merciful, and seeking justice for each and all.

A Faith That Is Logically Coherent

Second, the elements of a faith should be logically coherent. A trustworthy faith is not simply a collection of preferences picked up as you make your way from one chapter to another, much as you pick up items from a cafeteria serving line. The parts of a living faith should be consistent with one another, so that each part works with the others and none of the parts work against another (or against the whole). You cannot trust a faith that contains contradictions.

A Faith That Is Seriously Believable

Third, a faith should be "seriously believable," that is, in your heart of hearts you should be able to believe that what you say is true in real life.[2] You need to believe that God can do what you say God can do. Responsible Christians think about the extent and character of God's power, and articulate a faith in which they are confident that God truly acts in the world in the way that they say God acts.

An individual or community needs to consider what it believes in the light of real life experience. When you pray, for instance, you should believe that God can *really* act in the way that you request in prayer. When a community prays for God to change a particular situation, the congregation needs to meditate on whether the situation actually changes in the way that the community prayed, and, if so, whether they are confident that God was the agent of change. If the situation does not change, then the community needs to consider explanations for why it did not change or to reconsider its notion of prayer.

A Faith That Calls for the Moral Treatment of All People and Elements of Nature

In addition to these basic criteria, a faith should call for the moral treatment of all human beings and all elements of the natural world. To illustrate again from my own faith, I believe that God calls us to love our neighbors as ourselves. By "neighbors" I have in mind everything in the world—human beings, animals, and other elements of nature. Recognizing that love can take different forms in different circumstances, a mature faith should lead a person or a group to express as much love as possible for every neighbor in every situation in life. Indeed, a mature faith should help you recognize God's unconditional love as the basis for your own self-understanding, and it should empower you to accept yourself while calling you to want to live less for yourself and more for God.

FORMULATING A FAITH OF YOUR OWN

You can articulate a summary of your faith in a number of ways. Obviously, you can use words in straightforward ways, much as I have in this book, attempting to say in clear propositions what you believe. You can move in the direction of poetry or even the arts. I have seen statements of faith in the form of musical compositions, drawings and paintings, PowerPoint presentations (utilizing pictures), fabric arts, sculpture, and dance. These latter media are especially useful for communicating aspects of awareness and faith that cannot be expressed satisfactorily in straightforward propositions.

At the same time, as I said in the Introduction, we need to push as far as we can to say plainly what we believe. If you decide to express your faith in a medium other than propositional-style language, I urge you to accompany your artistic expression with a commentary that states your basic convictions as directly as you can. That way, your conversation partners will have a better opportunity to help you reflect on the degree to which your faith is in continuity with the Bible and Christian tradition, is logically coherent, is seriously believable, and is morally responsible.

Two possible ways of articulating your own faith are set forth in the following paragraphs. Both continue the style I have used in this volume of encouraging you to speak or write as clearly and straightfor-wardly as possible.

Writing Your Own Credo

Students in theological seminary are often required to write a "credo." The word *credo* is a Latin word that literally means, "I believe." A credo is a relatively brief and straightforward statement of what a person believes. Taking its cue from the structure of several of the historic affirmations of faith, a credo often sets out what the speaker or writer believes according to the categories of this book: God, Jesus Christ, the Holy Spirit, the Trinity, for example.

Using the outline that follows, I recommend that you write a series of nine statements that each puts into a sentence or two what you believe. You might draw from the perspectives that are set out in this book, especially making use of the conclusions that you made as you read each chapter and considered the Questions for Discussion at the end. Or, you might set forth ideas you have found elsewhere, or your own ideas.

One easy possibility is to begin each of your statements with the words " I believe," in ways such as the following:

1. I believe that we formulate our interpretations of Christian faith by drawing on the following resources . . . . [Beyond simply listing the resources, you will likely find it helpful to say something about how you conceive each one. For example, if you look to the Bible as a resource for formulating your faith, you might briefly describe how you understand the Bible.]
2. I believe in a God who . . . .
3. I believe that Jesus Christ is . . . .
4. I believe that the Holy Spirit is . . . .
5. I believe in the Trinity as . . . . (Note: If you do not believe in the Trinity, you might omit this item.)
6. I believe that God's ultimate purposes are . . . .
7. I believe that the church is (put here a description of the nature of the church, e.g., "called by God"), and that the purpose of the church is . . . .
8. I believe that evil is . . . .
9. I believe that the relationship of the church to other religions is . . . .

If the format of "I believe . . ." is too repetitious or inflexible for you, you might employ different words to introduce at least some of the ideas. You might also add an extra sentence or two to some of the categories to fill out your thought.

You might take your cue from the National Public Radio series "This I Believe," in which people from all walks of life employ a variety of formats to set out their most important values. Some offer propositions in styles similar to the one I just described. Others recount autobiographical experiences that summarize what they believe. Some contributors describe other people who exemplify what the contributors believe—teachers, coworkers, church members, even strangers with whom they have casual encounters. One contribution took the form of a series of questions and answers (rather like some of the catechisms developed in and shortly after the Reformation), and another the form of a parable.

If you are doing this exercise as part of a study group, I hope you will share your credos with one another. One person could read her or his credo, and other members of the group could name points at which it seems strong and vibrant, ask questions, and suggest points at which the speaker or writer might want to think further.

To make matters even more interesting, you might get copies of the Apostles' Affirmation of Faith (or Creed), the Nicene Affirmation of Faith, and an affirmation of faith from the history of your church and one written in the contemporary setting. You could then go item by item and compare the affirmations of these different voices with your own.

Identifying the Elements of Your Own Faith

Another way of formulating the core of your own faith is to go through the perspectives that are discussed in this book and to indicate the ones that most adequately express your own faith. Below, I have simplified the list of possibilities for interpretation that are articulated in this book by grouping together ideas that are similar from the sections on understandings in the Bible, the history of the church, and the contemporary world. You might go through the list and check the possibilities that are most meaningful to you. I have added numbers to make it easier to discuss these possibilities with your conversation partners. A check mark in front of an item would indicate, "This idea is one of my choices." I have also added blank lines where you can write possibilities that may occur to you that are not included in this list.

It is sometimes possible to mark more than one interpretive possibility in each section below. After making your initial selections, you do need to go over them from the perspectives of the four criteria above (being in continuity with the Bible and Christian tradition, logically coherent, seriously believable, and moral).

Resources for Developing a Faith

1. _____ Direct communication from God
2. _____ Drawing from the Bible
3. _____ Reflection on experience (wisdom or natural theology)
4. _____ Discerning God's purposes through dialogue with tradition
5. _____ Scientific worldview
6. _____ Philosophy
7. _____ Popular religious expressions
8. _____ Other _____

God

9. ____A relational God who responds to the world
10. ____God as all-powerful
11. ____God as unmoved mover
12. ____Watchmaker God
13. ____A God with unlimited love but limited power
14. ____A nonpersonal God
15. ____Other _____

Jesus Christ

16. ____Prophet of the end-time: God's agent of the present and coming realm
17. ____One who reveals God
18. ____God in the flesh: the second person of the Trinity
19. ____Victor over evil
20. ____Makes substitutionary atonement (Anselm)
21. ____Affects humankind (Abelard)
22. ____The great example
23. ____Is coming again
24. ____Liberator
25. ____Leader of nonviolent resistance
26. ____Living presence, a friend who is always with us
27. ____Symbol of God
28. ____Sage and poet of God
29. ____Other _____

Holy Spirit

30. ____Preserves the energy of chaos; assists with creation; sustains creation; re-creates community
31. ____Fills people with ecstasy: the Pentecostal experience
32. ____The Spirit supersedes sacred tradition (Montanus)
33. ____The third person of the Trinity: the Lord and giver of life, who proceeds from the Father and the Son
34. ____The sanctifier, who leads people in the holy life
35. ____The Spirit works through social process
36. ____The feminine dimension of God
37. ____Other _____

The Trinity

38. _____ The Trinity is present in the Bible
39. _____ The Trinity is not present in the Bible
40. _____ God adopted Jesus, the human being (adoptionism)
41. _____ Jesus was divine but God created him before the creation of the world (Arianism)
42. _____ God appeared in three different modes, one at a time (Modalism)
43. _____ God and Jesus are one (Binitarianism)
44. _____ The church in the West: God is one in substance while being three persons
45. _____ The church in the East: The Spirit proceeds only from the Father
46. _____ One God: one person (Unitarianism)
47. _____ Jesus is God (oneness Pentecostalism)
48. _____ Two Gods, but one in purpose (bitheism)
49. _____ Three Gods but one in purpose (tritheism)
50. _____ Other _____

God's Ultimate Purposes

51. _____ God aims for people to have a blessed life in the present
52. _____ The future (and present) realm of God
53. _____ The self follows the way to God in heaven
54. _____ Limited salvation
55. _____ Universal salvation
56. _____ Union with God: the Orthodox perspective
57. _____ Purgatory: a Roman Catholic touch
58. _____ Death is the end of human consciousness—period
59. _____ Figurative language and limited language: heaven and hell, the second coming
60. _____ Premillennialism (Christ will return before the thousand-year millennial reign)
61. _____ God's ultimate purposes as liberation from oppression (racial/ethnic, gender, political, economic, etc.)
62. _____ Consciousness is alive forever in God
63. _____ Other _____

The Church

64. ____Church as community of the realm
65. ____Church as sphere of heaven on earth/as doorway to the way to heaven above
66. ____The makeup of the church: predestination
67. ____The makeup of the church: free will
68. ____Church as ark to prepare the soul for the journey to heaven
69. ____Church as chaplain to the dominant culture
70. ____Church as alternative social order
71. ____Church as waiting room for the second coming of Jesus
72. ____Church as transforming the social world through direct engagement
73. ____Other _____

Evil

74. ____God pronounced a general curse on the world in response to human disobedience
75. ____Satan, demons, and the powers are responsible for evil
76. ____Evil results from idolatry
77. ____Suffering can serve God's purposes
78. ____Evil is necessary for growth
79. ____Evil is the absence of the good
80. ____Evil is an illusion
81. ____Human beings and others do not respond to the divine lure
82. ____Protest against
83. ____Other _____

Christianity and Other Religions

84. ____Christianity is the only true religion
85. ____All religions are essentially the same
86. ____Religions have evolved: different religions are at different stages
87. ____Each religion has its own integrity: peaceful coexistence
88. ____Religions cause one another to change
89. ____Judaism is a religion with full standing before God
90. ____Islam is a religion with full standing before God
91. ____Other _____

Notes

Introduction

1. I have been helped greatly in both the general structure of this book and in dealing with specific theological issues by Burton Z Cooper and John S. McClure, *Claiming Theology in the Pulpit* (Louisville, KY: Westminster John Knox Press, 2003).

2. From the standpoints of church tradition and academic theology, this book is a work on Christian doctrine or systematic theology. These terms refer to the attempt to set out a systematic statement of core theological convictions in such a way as to show how they relate with one another. Chapter 2, for instance, is on the doctrine of God. The best single work of systematic theology that I know is Clark M. Williamson, *Way of Blessing, Way of Life: A Christian Theology* (St. Louis: Chalice Press, 1999).

3. Clayton Schmitt, *Too Deep for Words: A Theology of Liturgical Expression* (Louisville, KY: Westminster John Knox Press, 2002).

Chapter 1: Resources for Developing a Faith

1. On one level wisdom refers to the capacity to discern God's designs. In addition, biblical writers sometimes personified wisdom as a woman who continues to act in the world to reveal God's ways and to warn human beings against folly. (For wisdom personified, see Prov. 1:20–33; 8:22–36.)

2. Most scholars think many in the Jewish community began to recognize a collection of biblical materials that are pretty much what Christians have adapted as the Old Testament in the period 70 to 135 CE, perhaps about the year 90 (at a place called Jamnia or Yavne). The New Testament was not proposed with the content that we have today until the year 367 CE, and formally accepted at synods soon after.

3. A corollary movement in philosophy (called rationalism) sought to establish unquestioned first principles from which other knowledge could be deduced.

Chapter 2: God

1. Discussion of God's character and power also often involves God's purposes, by which Christians have in mind what God intends for us as individuals,

for communities (including the church), and for the world of nature. I take up God's purposes in chapter 6.

2. Consideration of God's character sometimes takes place in the language of God's nature. Theologians, for instance, often discuss the nature of God, referring to what God is like in God's own being.

3. The library of sources that is contained in the Bible contains several major schools of thought: the Elohists, the Yahwists, the Deuteronomists, the priests, the wisdom writers, apocalypticism, and Hellenistic Judaism. A bird's-eye view of these schools of theology is found in Ronald J. Allen, *Preaching Is Believing: The Sermon as Theological Reflection* (Louisville, KY: Westminster John Knox Press, 2002), 38–44.

4. Justice is the social form of love. In a just world, all circumstances and actions are loving.

5. Or one could say that God has changeless and changeable aspects.

6. Paul Tillich, *Systematic Theology: Three Volumes in One* (Chicago: University of Chicago Press, 1967), vol. 1, 186–189.

Chapter 3: Jesus Christ

1. Albert Schweitzer, *The Quest of the Historical Jesus,* trans. W. Montgomery (1910; repr. Mineola, NY: Dover Publications, 2005).

2. We often speak the expression "Jesus Christ" as if it were two names, like Tom Smith. Jesus is a personal name (like Tom), but Christ is a title (messiah). The New Testament contains a number of different titles for Jesus. Among the most frequent are: Christ, Son of God, Son of Man, Lord, Savior, Son of David.

3. Some interpreters think that calling Jesus "Lord" is the same as identifying Jesus as God, since the Old Testament uses the designation Lord for God. I discuss this issue further in chapter 5, "The Trinity." For now, it is enough to report that I do not find this argument convincing.

4. Discussion of the death of Christ is often subsumed under the title "atonement." However, the term atonement has a particular meaning that does not always apply to interpretations of the death of Christ. This general subject is thus better discussed under the general heading "the meaning of the death of Christ," with atonement as a subcategory of that general conversation.

5. Scholars debate whether some texts depict Jesus' death as expiation (freeing people from sin) or propitiation (turning away God's anger). Few scholars today think that the New Testament presents Jesus' death as appeasing God's anger (propitiation).

6. As noted previously, we explore the notion of the Trinity further in chapter 5.

7. A twist on this viewpoint that has been quite popular is penal substitution. God is a holy and righteous judge. If God's laws are broken, God must punish the offenders. The sacrifice of Christ satisfies the legal requirement for punishment.

Chapter 4: The Holy Spirit

1. After the close of the biblical period, the church declared that the Spirit is the third member of the Trinity, but Christian thinkers debate whether the biblical witness itself pictures the Spirit as a member of the Trinity—a subject we discuss in chapter 5.

2. Some Christians speak of the Holy Spirit as "the liberating Spirit" because they see the essential work of the Spirit as leading the way in personal, social, political, and economic liberation.

3. Some Pentecostals, however, think that the experience of the Spirit is necessary for salvation, while others (as in the text above) think that the baptism of the Spirit is enriching but not ultimately necessary for salvation.

Chapter 5: The Trinity

1. E.g., Reginald Heber, "Holy, Holy, Holy," *Chalice Hymnal* (St. Louis: Chalice Press, 1995), no. 4.

2. The altered text is found in *Christian Worship: A Hymnal* (St. Louis: Christian Board of Publication, 1941), no. 107.

3. Other texts that Christians sometimes cite as pointing to the Trinity include the following that mention God, Christ, and the Holy Spirit: Rom. 14:17–18; 15:16; 1 Cor. 6:11; 12:4–6; 2 Cor. 1:21–22; Gal. 4:6; Eph. 2:17–22; 3:14–19; 1 Thess. 1:3–5; 2 Thess. 2:13–14; 1 Tim. 3:16; Titus 3:4–6; 1 Pet. 1:1–2. But most scholars agree that these passages presume God as sovereign, working through Christ and the Holy Spirit as agents. These passages assume unity of purpose among God, Christ, and Spirit while not claiming that the three are one being.

4. Another popular interpretation is that the word "us" was the royal "we" (as when a monarch says, "We welcome you to our court"). However, this way of speaking is not paralleled elsewhere in antiquity.

5. Philo, "On Dreams," 1:229, in *Philo,* trans. F.H. Colson and G.H. Whitaker, Loeb Classical Library (Cambridge: Harvard University Press, 1968), 5:419. See further Philo, "Questions and Answers on Genesis," 2:62, *Philo Supplement: I. Questions and Answers on Genesis,* trans. Ralph Marcus, Loeb Classical Library (Cambridge: Harvard University Press, 1979), 151.

6. In the interest of inclusive language, elsewhere in this book I try to avoid calling God Father and referring to Christ as the Son. When discussing the Trinity, however, which speaks of one God in three persons (Father, Son, and Holy Spirit), it is sometimes useful to use the designations Father and Son. As we have already noted, in the strict sense God is not masculine in gender, but is either inclusive of both genders or beyond gender. While the earthly Jesus was a male, the resurrected Christ (according to apocalyptic theology) is beyond gender.

7. Patripassianism is from Latin words meaning father (patri, from *pater*) and suffer (passus- from verb *pati*).

8. Orthodox churches today do not say the phrase "and the Son" when confessing the Nicene Affirmation of Faith.

9. The essential Trinity is sometimes called the ontological Trinity, or the immanent Trinity. The word "ontological" is derived from Greek and means thinking about ("logical") being or essence ("onto"). The word immanent means indwelling.

10. Oneness Pentecostalism is sometimes known as "Jesus Only," but many Oneness Pentecostals view this term as too easily leading to misinterpretation, or even as perjorative (when used by outsiders to speak of the Oneness movement).

Chapter 6: God's Ultimate Purposes

1. The technical theological name for God's ultimate purposes is eschatology, which comes from two Greek words meaning "word" (*logos*) and "last things" (*eschatos*). In technical use, the term eschatology refers not just to the last things chronologically, but to God's ultimate purposes.

2. For formulations of the covenants, see Gen. 12:1–3; chaps. 15; 17 (covenant with Sarah and Abraham); Exod., chaps 19–24 (covenant with Moses); and 2 Sam. 7:1–17 (covenant with David). Note also Gen. 8:20–22 (covenant with all peoples). The wisdom literature is not centered in a covenant, but that literature presupposes the same general understanding of God's ultimate purposes, namely, that people should live a secure and prosperous life in the present, as in Prov. 3:1–26; 31:10–31.

3. Among representative passages are Ps. 6:5; 88:3–6; 89:46–48; Isa. 38:10–18.

4. The idea of God's ultimate purposes extending beyond the present world into another sphere of life began to emerge in Israel only with Isa. 56–66 and Zech. 9–14 (both written after about 520 BCE).

5. For example: Rom. 8:18–25; 1 Cor. 15:35–49; Mark, chap. 13; Matt. 24:1–44; Luke 21:5–33; James 5:7–12; 2 Peter 3:1–10; Rev. 20:1–22:7

6. At the time the New Testament was written, Jewish people sometimes mixed the two viewpoints just described—the expectation that God would bring a new world and the hope that the essence of the self would ascend to heaven. Consequently, Christians today need to be careful not to oversimplify biblical perspectives.

7. An important issue is what is meant by the term "salvation." In popular discussion, salvation usually refers to being ultimately and finally joined to God, either in heaven or in the new-world-realm-of-God. In this chapter, I use it more broadly to refer to God's ultimate purposes.

8. Many passages in the Old Testament assert that God actively wishes to bless all peoples, including Gentiles. See, e.g., Isa. 25:6–10; 42:6–7; 44:1–5; 45:20–25; 49:1–6; 55:1–5. In these instances, God seeks to bless every human community in the present.

9. Julian of Norwich, *Showings,* trans. James Walsh. The Classics of Western Spirituality (New York: Paulist Press, 1978), 151.

10. I also hear people use the notion of hell in a confused way. In Christian tradition, hell refers specifically to punishment that results from unfaithfulness. But increasingly I hear people use the language of hell to speak of any situation of suffering, including many situations that do not result from unfaithfulness.

11. This movement is sometimes known as dispensational premillennialism, or simply dispensationalism.

12. There are two popular forms of premillennialism, which differ in their understanding of the relationship of the millennium and the tribulation—a period of intense suffering. (1) Pretribulation premillennialists believe that Christ will return and rapture the church (that is, take the members of the church to be with him). A tribulation (period of intense suffering in the world) will take place, followed by the millennium, and then the final return of Christ and final judgment. (2) Post-tribulation premillennialists believe that the tribulation will take place, and then Christ will return to establish the millennium, after which the final return and final judgment will take place.

Chapter 7: The Church

1. A church's understanding of its nature and purpose is tied to its understanding of God's ultimate purposes (discussed in the preceding chapter).

2. Space does not allow consideration of several issues that have become central to church discussion over the centuries, such as the meaning of baptism, the breaking of the bread and the drinking of the cup, and ministerial leadership.

3. I should be clear that other kinds of churches also oppose these conditions and work to free individuals and communities from them.

Chapter 8: Evil

1. Christians have often said that the serpent was Satan. In the book of Genesis itself the serpent is not Satan, but is an ordinary creature not satisfied with that role who seeks an elevated place in the world similar to that of God.

2. The death of Jesus does not effect salvation in and of itself, but becomes salvifically significant when it is connected with the resurrection.

3. The devil has come to be known by a variety of popular designations, including Satan, Beelzebub, Prince of the (This) World, and Lucifer. Less well known but still in use: Adversary, Dragon, Evil One, Mephistopheles, Old Scratch, Tempter, and Wicked One.

4. The origin of this picture is unclear. Someone may have adapted the horns from figures from Greek mythology who had horns. Satan is sometimes pictured having half the body of an animal, in a way similar to the satyr, a half-human and half-goat figure in Greek mythology. Another possibility is that the horns came

from non-Christian horned deities and the practice among some non-Christians of wearing headpieces that had horns.

5. John Hick, *Evil and the God of Love*, rev. ed. (New York: Palgrave Macmillan, 2007).

6. John K. Roth, "A Theodicy of Protest," in *Encountering Evil: Live Options in Theodicy*, rev. ed., ed. Stephen T. Davis (Louisville, KY: Westminster John Knox Press, 2001), 2–22.

Chapter 9: Christianity and Other Religions

1. These categories are taken directly from Burton Z Cooper and John S. McClure, *Claiming Theology for the Pulpit* (Louisville, KY: Westminster John Knox Press, 2003).

Final Exercise

1. David L. Tracy, *Blessed Rage for Order: The New Pluralism in Theology* (New York: Seabury Press, 1975), 64–71. Building on Tracy's insight, my colleague Clark M. Williamson proposes three excellent criteria for assessing the adequacy of any statement: appropriateness to one's deepest convictions about God, intelligibility, and moral plausibility. See Clark M. Williamson, *Way of Blessing, Way of Life: A Christian Theology* (St. Louis: Chalice Press, 1999), 77–88. For one of my own formulations, see Ronald J. Allen, *Preaching: An Essential Guide* (Nashville: Abingdon Press, 2002), 49–58. The use of these criteria, of course, depends on being clearly aware of one's core theological convictions. I have simplified and adapted these criteria for the three criteria suggested for assessing one's own faith in the present book.

2. For the criterion of "seriously believable," though formulated as "seriously imaginable," see David Kelsey, *The Uses of Scripture in Recent Theology* (Philadelphia: Fortress Press, 1975), 170–174. For a crisp statement of this criterion as "intelligibility," see Williamson, *Way of Blessing, Way of Life,* 86–88.

Selected Bibliography

This brief bibliography lists some sample volumes that discuss the major topics of the present book and many more. Two types of books are listed: dictionaries of theological terms and systematic theologies. Books are listed alphabetically by author, and not by order of preference.

Dictionaries of Theology

A dictionary of theology contains short articles that define important words that are important in the Bible and in Christian thinking.

González, Justo L. *Essential Theological Terms.* Louisville, KY: Westminster John Knox Press, 2005. Brief summaries of basic theological terms. The reader can get started by looking up Scripture, Reason and Truth, Faith and Reason, Christology, Incarnation, Spirit (Holy), Trinity, Eschatology, Eternal Life, Kingdom of God, Heaven, Theodicy (evil).

McKim, Donald K. *Westminster Dictionary of Theological Terms.* Louisville, KY: Westminster John Knox Press, 1996. Brief summaries of a wide range of theological terms, including many variations. You might sample this book by looking at the groups of terms that are associated with God, Jesus, Holy Spirit, the Trinity, church, eschatology, and evil. In each case, the author provides short, pithy articles on multiple perspectives on the topic.

Systematic Theologies

A systematic theology is a book (or series of books) that presents many scholars' religious (theological) convictions in a systematic manner. The volumes below were selected because they can be easily read and because they represent a range of religious views. Whereas *A Faith of Your Own* presents options, most of these volumes develop specific viewpoints, often in dialogue with many of the options depicted in this volume.

vans, James H. Jr. *We Have Been Believers: An African American Systematic Theology.* Minneapolis: Augsburg, 1992. Basic Christian beliefs from the perspective of African American experience.

Grenz, Stanley J. *Theology for the Community of God.* Grand Rapids: Wm. B. Eerdmans Publishing Co., 2000. An irenic evangelical enters into conversation with multiple points of view in both historical and contemporary periods.

Guthrie, Shirley C. *Christian Doctrine.* Rev. ed., Louisville, KY: Westminster John Knox Press, 1994. Very clear summary of traditional Christian teaching in conversation with other viewpoints.

Johnson, Elizabeth A. *She Who Is: The Mystery of God in Feminist Theological Discourse.* New York: Herder & Herder, 2002. An interpretation of Christian doctrines from the perspective of women's experience.

Jones, Joe R. *A Grammar of Christian Faith: Systematic Explorations in Christian Life and Doctrine.* 2 vols. Lanham, MD: Rowman & Littlefield Pubs., 2002. Written from the perspective that the language and practices of the church shape our faith.

McGrath, Alister E. *Christian Theology: An Introduction.* 4th ed. Malden, MA: Blackwell Publishing Co., 2007. Theologically middle of the road, with attention to ideas and figures from church history and today.

Morse, Christopher. *Not Every Spirit: A Dogmatics of Christian Disbelief.* Philadelphia: Trinity Press International, 1994. Intriguing approach, helping believers recognize that every affirmation also means that one denies certain things.

Schüssler Fiorenza, Francis, and John P. Galvin. *Systematic Theology: Roman Catholic Perspectives.* Minneapolis: Fortress Press, 2000. As the subtitle implies, this work sets out Roman Catholic perspectives.

Sobrino, Jon, and Ignacio Ellacuria, eds. *Systematic Theology: Perspectives from Liberation Theology.* Maryknoll, NY: Orbis Books, 1996. Several authors write individual articles on foundational themes from the point of view of social, political, economic, and religious liberation.

Thorsen, Don. *An Exploration of Christian Theology.* Peabody, MA: Hendrickson Pubs., 2008. The author surveys multiple viewpoints in Christian doctrine. Evangelical in orientation, with a wide range of perspectives.

Williamson, Clark M. *Way of Blessing, Way of Life: A Christian Theology.* St. Louis: Chalice Press, 1999. From the perspective of life as continuous process and a limited God, with attention to the concerns of women, Jewish-Christian relationships, and the environment. In my view, the best statement of systematic theology.

Williams, J. Rodman, *Renewal Theology: Systematic Theology from a Charismatic Perspective.* 3 vols. in 1. Grand Rapids: Zondervan Publishing House, 1996. Systematic discussion of Christian doctrine from Pentecostal/charismatic point of view.

green
press
INITIATIVE

Presbyterian Publishing is committed to preserving ancient forests and natural resources. We elected to print this title on 30% post consumer recycled paper, processed chlorine free. As a result, for this printing, we have saved:

7 Trees (40' tall and 6-8" diameter)
2 Million BTUs of Total Energy
641 Pounds of Greenhouse Gases
3,089 Gallons of Wastewater
188 Pounds of Solid Waste

Presbyterian Publishing made this paper choice because our printer, Thomson-Shore, Inc., is a member of Green Press Initiative, a nonprofit program dedicated to supporting authors, publishers, and suppliers in their efforts to reduce their use of fiber obtained from endangered forests.

For more information, visit www.greenpressinitiative.org

Environmental impact estimates were made using the Environmental Defense Paper Calculator. For more information visit: www.edf.org/papercalculator